REVIVE

REVIVE

How to Transform Traditional Businesses into Digital Leaders

JASON ALBANESE

BRIAN MANNING

Publisher: Paul Boger
Editor-in-Chief: Amy Neidlinger
Acquisitions Editor: Charlotte C. Maiorana
Cover Designer: Chuti Prasertsith
Managing Editor: Kristy Hart
Project Editor: Andy Beaster
Copy Editor: Cenveo® Publisher Services
Proofreader: Cenveo Publisher Services
Indexer: Cenveo Publisher Services
Compositor: Cenveo Publisher Services
Manufacturing Buyer: Dan Uhrig

© 2016 by Jason Albanese and Brian Manning
Published by Pearson Education, Inc.
Old Tappan, New Jersey 07675

For information about buying this title in bulk quantities, or for special sales opportunities (which may include electronic versions; custom cover designs; and content particular to your business, training goals, marketing focus, or branding interests), please contact our corporate sales department at corpsales@pearsoned.com or (800) 382-3419.

For government sales inquiries, please contact governmentsales@pearsoned.com.

For questions about sales outside the U.S., please contact international@pearsoned.com.

Company and product names mentioned herein are the trademarks or registered trademarks of their respective owners.

Printed in the United States of America

First Printing November 2015

ISBN-10: 0-13-430643-0
ISBN-13: 978-0-13-430643-8

Pearson Education LTD.
Pearson Education Australia PTY, Limited
Pearson Education Singapore, Pte. Ltd.
Pearson Education Asia, Ltd.
Pearson Education Canada, Ltd.
Pearson Educación de Mexico, S.A. de C.V.
Pearson Education—Japan
Pearson Education Malaysia, Pte. Ltd.

Library of Congress Control Number: 2015949478

From Jason Albanese:
To those who inspire me most—My amazing wife, Emily, whose dedication to our children at home and her students in the classroom leaves me speechless. And my two incredible boys Charlie and Henry, their passion for knowledge and incredible imagination remind me there is always more to learn. I cherish every moment I spend with the three of you.

From Brian Manning:
To my parents, Marie and Steve, whose work ethic and encouragement have been my biggest inspiration to achieve more than I ever thought possible. And to my wife Amrita—whose spirit and passion for adventure makes it all worthwhile.

Contents at a Glance

Contents

Acknowledgments

We would like to thank the entire team at Centric Digital, without whom this book would never have been written. If it was not their intellect, passion, advice, and support, we would not have the knowledge, exposure, or insights necessary to put this book together, and we certainly would not have had the time. Special thanks to Leslie Knauer, Ezequiel Gorbano, Ezequiel Riquelme, and the entire management team at Centric Digital—Brian Dearth, Brendan Hammond, Robert Levine, Stephen Morrissey, Jean-Marcel Nicolai, David Palmieri, and Pratiksha Patel.

About the Authors

JASON ALBANESE is CEO & Co-Founder of Centric Digital, a leading digital transformation solutions company. His vision and entrepreneurial skills accumulated during a successful career building innovative B2B digital companies has allowed him to turn Centric Digital into one of the fastest growing companies in America. Previously, he co-founded and served as CEO of SageSecure LLC, a digital asset management and risk company that also succeeded in delivering strategic growth to the Fortune® 1000 through digital products and services. Albanese writes a weekly business strategy column for INC .com, is author of *Network Security Illustrated* (McGraw-Hill, 2003), has been published in *The Journal of Research and Practice in Information Technology (JRPIT)*, and holds a patent on an Internet-based distance learning system he co-designed. He serves as the Chair of the Governance Committee on the board of Partnership with Children, a non-profit focused on outreach to New York City public school students at risk of academic failure; and is an active member of Young Presidents Organization, serving on the board of YPO Manhattan in the role of Member Integration Committee chair.

BRIAN MANNING is President, Chief Digital Officer & Co-Founder of Centric Digital. He has leveraged his deep digital expertise and creativity to shape Centric Digital's brand and market position into the strategic partner of choice for the world's largest enterprises. Manning started his career at Accenture and since went on to lead digital businesses within global enterprises, such as Citigroup and spinoffs such as Barnes & Noble.com. He has managed $500+MM e-commerce businesses, defined multi-billion dollar consumer digital bank strategies, and launched dozens of digital products. Manning's passion for all things digital sets a high bar for Centric Digital's clients, partners and employees. Chief Digital Officers consistently seek his advice and he has helped shape the digital organizations and strategies of several Fortune 500 companies. In addition to driving thought leadership for Centric Digital he is a frequent guest writer drawing the connection between the latest trends that traditional enterprises can leverage. His quest for doing everything digitally has defined Centric Digital's operations and fully removed the use of paper from his work or personal life.

Introduction

Many thought leaders point out major theories and ideas as to how digital has impacted business, the economy, and society. That's helpful, but this book will do that and more. It will show you "how to" transform or build a core business model that is ready for the digital age. This is not a book about chasing the latest technology, but instead it is a book on strategy, business models, and the art and science of creating your own digital transformation. Our goal is to help you change the game before it changes you, while providing you with the initial thought processes, guidance, and "how-to" so you can.

Digital is about immediacy—about getting the word out, and making changes. Oddly enough, the digital transformation process itself can take years—especially if you have a large company. Why? Because it's not just your business model that may need to change. It's also your people, your technology platforms, and your operational processes that also have to change. Conceiving a new business model and implementing a technology capable of disrupting your industry is only part of the challenge. It's harder to create the teams, the processes and the change that the new technology and model requires. But we will show you how to do that too.

Today, companies are asking most often how to drive the kind of change that will get them noticed, that will put them ahead in their industry and that will make them the next great case study. Are you debating, embarking on a major transformation? Are you worried about whether the idea, or the risk of change will fly in your

1990s	2000s	TODAY
The mall	Amazon.com	Amazon & (Every Store).com
Tower Records, Radio	iTunes, Sirius XM	Spotify, Pandora
Blockbuster	OnDemand	Netflix
Barnes & Noble	Books Shipped Same Day	The Kindle
Desktops	Laptops	Tablets
Cell phone	Blackberry	iPhone/Android
E-tickets	Printable tickets	Mobile Boarding Pass
Bank branches	ATM deposit	Mobile Check Deposit
Rental cars	-	Zipcar
Supermarket	-	Fresh Direct, Blue Apron
Real estate broker	Craiglist	Zillow
Car Service	-	Uber
Timeshare	-	AirBnB
Kodak	Email Photos	Instagram, Facebook
Recruiters	HotJobs	LinkedIn
File Cabinet	Portable Drive	Google Drive, Box.com
Zagats, Reservations, Delivery	Menupages	Yelp, Open Table, Seamless
Travel Agent	Travelocity	TripAdvisor

Figure 0.1 Digital disruptions

current company culture? Today, conservative and cautious can kill your long-term opportunities. If you do nothing else around digital transformation this year, read this book. At minimum, it should help you recognize digital disruptions that will be or are a threat to your business, similar to relatively recent examples outlined in Figure 0.1.

Your customers are in the driver's seat because they know what they want or they've come to know what they want through researching on the Internet, and then go after those companies that deliver the user experiences they are seeking. That's why upstarts have been able to raise billions on inflated valuations creating some of the most highly-valued private tech companies of all time.

What drove their success? *Customers.* Because the traditional model was ineffective, costly, and a bad customer experience, they flocked to these new startups when they came on the scene—not because of their app, but because of their unique business model, made possible by digital.

You don't have to be an analyst, a statistician, an IT geek, a technology guru, or a social media master to take on a transformation initiative. You, however, have to understand the three key drivers of transformation:

1. Changing technologies
2. Competition
3. Changing customer demand for more technology that actually makes their lives better

But most companies aren't moving as quickly as they probably should to leverage the power of digital, which is becoming more and more a necessity to stay competitive. This was evident in November 2011 when a three-year study conducted by the MIT Center for Digital Business and Capgemini Consulting concluded that globally, only one-third of companies had an effective digital transformation program in place.[1] Then in 2014 the Altimeter Group conducted a survey where participants were given a definition of digital transformation to read beforehand. Afterward, they were asked whether their company was undergoing a formal digital transformation that year. While 88 percent of executives and digital strategists stated that they were, only 25 percent of those claiming a transformation had actually mapped out their digital-customer journey—even after reading the definition.

Digital transformation is not just about data, numbers, studies, surveys, and technology. To better understand it, we need to look closely at the stories behind digital transformations and the companies that get affected, both positively and negatively. Companies overcome competition by creating better customer experiences. Other companies get challenged because they are not proactive. We will provide you with a primer to create, develop, and manage your own digital transformation effectively so you end up on the right side of all that digital has to offer.

---

[1] https://www.capgemini.com/resource-file-access/resource/pdf/The_Digital_Advantage__How_Digital_Leaders_Outperform_their_Peers_in_Every_Industry.pdf

This book will explore and illustrate how companies can change, engage, interact with, and disrupt the current digital ecosystem. For those of you who may have forgotten high-school biology, an ecosystem includes all the living things in a given area that interact with each other and their environment.

Many companies may include "new website design," or "incorporating social media" into their websites and consider that "digital transformation." Statements like, "We need to redesign our website, we need to build a mobile app" are not strategies, they are implementations of what should be delivering on a strong digital business strategy. These tactics can enhance or be the outcome of the transformation, but they are not the transformation.

What this book, and our entire philosophical approach, is about is that digital transformation is the tip of the spear of your future business model. It's fundamental to your business and your business strategy. It has a seat at the boardroom table. It requires it's own profit and loss (P&L). Digital transformation is the heartbeat, the mantra, the thread that runs through this book.

In spite of thousands of examples where businesses of all sizes have successfully transformed, almost every company facing transformation will experience some internal resistance.

You don't have to be a marketing, branding, or business genius to realize what happens when your company doesn't keep up with trends in customer desires, needs or expectations. Need an example in one word? Kodak. Kodak management's inability to see digital photography as the future continued for decades. Even when the general public saw what was happening, Kodak's management didn't. As late as 2007, a few years before declaring bankruptcy, a Kodak marketing video told consumers that "Kodak is back" and that they weren't going to play anymore with digital. Even when studies showed digital would overtake Kodak's market, researchers there concluded it would "take at least 10 years" to do so.

Not everyone learned the lessons Kodak taught so many. Many companies still resist digital transformation the way Kodak resisted digital cameras. Even long-standing companies can transform themselves if they are willing to push past the internal resistance.

If you and your organization are ready to transform, what are the steps you can start to take? First, address the resistance. Stop talking about digital as if it's something separate, or a channel of your business instead of at its core. Begin ingraining digital thinking into everything you do. Make it part of your culture, business strategy, and model. Make it a primary touchpoint of your business. Make digital transformation core to your business strategy.

For older and more traditional companies, digital is a separate shared-service unit. This is usually the right structure for companies with less digital maturity. Ultimately, digital will need to be a part of every part of the business, similar to how Amazon or Google may think about digital within their organization—where there is no separate digital team. Businesses won't have "digital teams" because everything will have digital embedded in it.

Second, identify your company's expertise, talent, and uniqueness. Digital transformation is not about simply implementing "best practices" or attempting to copy the digital pure-play companies that are already out there. It's about understanding *your* digital DNA.

Third, create a digital transformation vision. Bill Gates had a vision when he started Microsoft. He envisioned that there would be a computer on every desk in every home long before many people knew what a computer was. Have a vision for the future of business whereby leverage is digital. Digital is the core of every business that operates more effectively with better integrity, and more transparency. They better serve their community and society, and the environment.

Fourth, have fun. Digital transformation shouldn't be this big, heavy, change initiative. Make it fun and exciting for your employees to participate. It should be a challenging, fun, game changing initiative that gives your team purpose.

Fifth, create your own unique experience to get the edge in your market. Nike did it. Disney did it. Casper Sleep and Warby Parker did it.

This book will help show businesses of all sizes how to transform, how to become the digital leaders in their industry. Our hope is that you will stop talking about digital as if it's something separate from your business. Instead it should be seen as the primary touchpoint that both customers and employees connect with daily, because they do already for many reasons. Digital should be a seamless component of your company.

1

The Essence of Digital

Similar to the terms "the cloud" and "big data," the term digital is often misunderstood and seemingly limitless in scope. It can impact business strategy, user experiences, marketing channels, technology platforms, product development, human resources, communications, customer services, operations, and so on.

In short, any technology that connects people and machines with information or each other is *digital*, which means digital has become essential to every department in every business. When you're defining digital, it's a broad business concept, not just an emerging technology concept. Digital impacts most aspects of most businesses, including sales, marketing, customer service, operations, finance, supply chain, human resources, and so on.

Industrial Revolution Similarities

Digital is still in the early stages of what in the future could be looked back on as a change on the scale of the Industrial Revolution, when emerging technologies, new business models, and new processes of the time dramatically changed business, the environment, and society for the better. We believe digital is really today's Industrial Revolution that could have a similar order of magnitude impact on business, the environment, and society when it reaches maturity. Before getting into defining that digital is today, it may be helpful to explore the Industrial Revolution and compare to what is going on today in digital.

History is repeating itself, doing the same thing to the world with the "digital revolution" that the Industrial Revolution did with machines. The thing about the Industrial Revolution and the Digital Revolution is that while technologies change, people don't. The same dynamics that brought about the Industrial Revolution have brought about the Digital Revolution.

What most people know about the Industrial Revolution was that it created more products faster, more economically. Sound familiar? As we mentioned before, digital is about immediacy and satisfying what people always want—"faster, better, and cheaper." Even in the 1700s people wanted things faster, cheaper, and better.

The Industrial Revolution of the 1700s was similar to the Digital Revolution of today in that it impacted practically every phase of people's lives, created a higher standard of living, and brought about a lower cost for manufactured goods. It impacted social and economic change. Most importantly it forced people to think differently about how they engaged with the world. Before the Industrial Revolution, life was hard—it was about subsistence 24/7. One of the user needs that kick-started the Industrial Revolution was a pretty basic human one—clothes.

Prior to the Industrial Revolution, the average person may have owned a fraction of the clothing the average person would after. Cloth was a real luxury because cotton or wool had to be carded by hand, then spun by hand on a spinning wheel, and then put on a loom and woven by hand, before becoming fabric which was then sewn by hand. The entire process was very labor intensive.

Along the way to the birth of the Industrial Revolution, a series of innovations in the cloth manufacturing and thread spooling process were invented. These new technologies required less human energy, making fabric production easier, faster, and cheaper. Perhaps the greatest innovation at this time was the invention of a spinning engine called a Jenny (short for engine) in 1764. The Jenny enabled sewers to produce multiple spools of threads simultaneously, making the weaving process easier and faster because with more thread more people could weave more because they weren't spending weeks spinning thread. This gave them time to sew. In modern terms, we'd call this, "enhancing the consumer's experience."

Only 10 years later when James Hargreaves, the Jenny's inventor, passed away, there were more than 20,000 spinning Jennys in use across Britain. From here, other inventors improved upon Hargreaves' Jenny—producing bigger, faster, and cheaper models to operate spinning engines. Around the same time, someone else invented the power loom that mechanized the process of weaving cloth.

Someone else invented the steam engine and the process for casting iron, and then there was the invention of the telegraph, the stock exchange, and the railroad system. All these fantastic innovations ultimately contributed to what would become not only the fabric industry but the start of the Industrial Revolution. Everyone who invented something did so to solve a problem they were experiencing in their particular industry. But one person, Sir Richard Arkwright, an Englishman, saw the big picture and used what he saw to transform the world. Today we call him the "Father of the Industrial Revolution." Why?

Arkwright combined new technology, power, machinery, semiskilled labor, and the new raw material (cotton) to mass produce yarn. The fact that Arkwright combined new and existing technologies to produce what essentially became the first factory is why he's called the Father of the Industrial Revolution. This is a simple but, critically important, fact to remember because the ability to see, combine, and implement different technologies and processes is exactly what drives digital transformation.

Like the inventions of the Industrial Revolution, digital technologies are enabling businesses to transform themselves and do things in better way than before. The combinations of digital technology along with the new creative thinking around business that digital enables, allow us to create faster, cheaper, and better services and products. Companies can now replicate what Arkwright did for the world within their own industry—leveraging emerging technologies to create a better company. By creating their own industry-wide revolution, they bring innovation to a static economic ecosystem.

Just as the "Jenny" didn't exist in the early 1700s, the Internet didn't exist in the 50s. Someone invented the Jenny, then a mechanical loom and a way to cast iron tools, a transportation system, a delivery system, and so on. A couple of hundred years later someone invented the Internet, RFID chips, and then the smartphone and social media. The technologies kept changing, but the people didn't.

People always want and do find a way to do things better, faster, and cheaper. That was true 250 years ago during the beginning of the Industrial Revolution, and it will be true 250 years from today, arguably the early stages of the Digital Revolution.

How Digital Revolutionizes Business
Digital Is Core to Business

Digital today provides immediacy. It's about listening to what your markets want and need, and then creating business models and strategies that address those needs and wants quickly. Your markets demand responses now. What often "makes sense" to someone thinking logically doesn't apply to someone thinking viscerally. Transformation is all about being responsive versus reactive. All markets are constantly morphing—evolving through consumer-driven wants. Innovation most often starts in the field, not in a focus group.

Digital Breaks Down Business Silos

Digital is not a silo. It transcends the typical business models and profit and loss (P&L). It also transcends the traditional channel mix. Digital transformation impacts experiences, technology, and people. It may incorporate the usual, but it also transcends the usual business models and units. That's why it's so complex and hard for companies to get good at it.

People have to be involved in it on a day-to-day basis. When people say, "What is digital?" they don't know because the term is so broad, so generic, so all encompassing. We could be talking about marketing channels and digital business strategy and somebody else is talking about the design of the website. Digital is all of those things and so much more. Even though many people mistake it for a faster record keeping or tracking system (two-dimensional) that's not what the Internet of Things (IoT) or digital is. It's more than that.

What Sir Richard Arkwright saw in the 1700s was what today's digital transformers are seeing as well—the third and fourth dimensional potential of technology. The ability to digitally transform a company means going beyond just collecting big data. It means interpreting it, understanding what it's telling us, and seeing new ways to help end users interact with and engage with your company, products, and services as a result.

Digital Gives Customers (A Loud) Voice

Business is very different today. Release your products as soon as possible, or else you will start to lose customers rapidly away. For example, in the gaming industry, if you are piloting a new game in beta but are consistently delaying release, your customers will react negatively unless you are adequately responsive to them.

Customers are in control today because they can talk to each other about your brand through digital channels, where it's publicly visible to everybody. They can even be louder than the marketing division of that brand. They're the ones who are going to choose who they follow, what they buy, and what their experience will be. If you don't understand their pain and know how to give them what they want with the great customer experience they expect, they're going to find someone who will. Pre digital, it was easy for a giant company to just drown out any of that negative noise with marketing. Because there wasn't a forum or social network for consumers to voice concerns, or a way for people to come together and really get their opinions out, a bad customer experience wasn't a big deal unless the person managed to get the attention of the media.

Even then, the screams died pretty quickly. With the Internet, those screams and issues are preserved for eternity—along with your responses even down to the letters you write and actions you take, or don't take.

What happens in times of disruptive change is that traditional metrics like quality, durability, and longevity are either challenged or thrown out, and values like speed, low cost, efficiency, and immediacy become the bar by which all challengers are measured.

New innovative companies initially come into the competition in a small way, and traditional businesses may not see them as a threat because they don't have the established brand awareness. Traditional businesses may feel safe and underestimate the new company's potential by comparing their offering to what's already there. Then the new company expands their initial business model and leveraging their technology platform, or combines technologies and quickly become a clear threat.

What we see are many companies although successful, mistakenly value the things their customers don't particularly care about, instead of focusing on the things their customers really want. When the gap between what a company values and what their customers value gets too big, that's when competition move in. That's why digital leaders put their customers in more control. That's not a bad thing.

Digital Enables Big Bang Disruption

They call them "Big Bang Disruptors" because you don't see them coming as they may not even be coming from areas you consider your industry. Remember Sir Richard Arkwright combined different technologies from different industries to kick-start an entire revolution. To say that someone who doesn't even compete with you can be one of your biggest threats is not an exaggeration.

Remember the almost dominance of stand-alone GPS systems like Garmin, Magellan, and TomTom? They thought they were the only game in town and were just competing with each other—until every smartphone on the market came with GPS and free map apps like Google Maps. In an article, they wrote for the *Harvard Business Review*, Larry Downes and Paul F. Nunes, consultants at the Accenture Institute for High Performance, wrote: "But now entire product lines—whole markets—are being created or destroyed overnight. Disruptors can come out of nowhere and instantly be everywhere. Once launched, such disruption is hard to fight."

Digital technologies level the playing field and accelerate the pace of delivery of large scale innovations. Gordon Crovitz, writing for the *Wall Street Journal*, agrees. Crovitz said, "Powerful new technologies like cloud computing and big data allow entrepreneurs to develop products and services that are 'simultaneously better, cheaper, and more customized,' 'This isn't disruptive innovation. It's devastating innovation.'"

Few industries, if any, are immune to disruption. If your business is going to survive, you need to accept this reality. Twenty years ago who could have predicted that something as simple as a mobile phone would turn industries like home phones, pinball and arcade games, GPS devices, casinos, cameras and video, flashlights, travel agents, restaurant guides, and newspapers upside down?

Customer demand is also going to force changes in heavily regulated industries like pharmaceuticals, transportation, and energy. We've already seen regulated services like education, medicine, and law face change.

Innovation changes not only the way people do business but the rules about *how* we do business. It always has and it always will. Just about the time we learn the new rules, they change again. In 1995 Joseph L. Bower and Clayton M. Christensen's wrote an article for the *Harvard Business Review*, "Disruptive Technologies: Catching the Wave." The article taught us what we know about how to spot disruptors before they cripple or kill our business.

Bower and Christensen told businesses to "be on the lookout for upstarts that offer cheap substitutes to their products, capture new, low-end customers, and then gradually move upmarket to pick off higher-end customers." When disrupters do appear, like a few lone ants strolling across a kitchen counter, it's time to act quickly—either by acquiring them ASAP, or embracing similar technology and business models.

2

The Difference between Reactive and Transformative Digital

Digital transformation involves reimagining the business model, customer or user experience, and operational processes in a way that connects people with your brand, business, products, and services. It's also about connecting and engaging people through emerging technologies in ways that create deeper relationships with your customers for the long term. Therefore, creating lasting transformative digital capabilities requires you to build a customer-centric culture within your own organization. It's not a simple or easy process—but it's necessary to not only survive but to thrive in today's economy.

Defining Reactive Digital

Digitally *reactive* companies typically try to force a traditional strategy onto the Internet or play catch up by copying or creating a digital strategy in response to a competitor's digital success.

Some major differences between reactive digital and transformational digital can be demonstrated by the following examples:

Reactive	Transformative
Digital as a channel	Digital core to business
Business unit centric	Customer centric
Multiple channels	Omni-channel
One to many	Personalized
Redundant experiences	Integrated ecosystem
Spreadsheets	Real-time visualized data
Manual processes	Automated

Reactive	Transformative
IT department	Cloud centric
Linear and big bang	Agile and iterative

As an example, the traditional banking industry has mostly been digitally reactive. This is surprising because the banking industry has driven technology innovation such as electronic fund transfers, ATMs, etc. The explanation may be that these particular innovations were serving product silos where each has their own technology, infrastructure, and even marketing models—all typical of the digitally reactive company. The digital transformation needed for banks to lead is better integration between product silos and presenting "one face" to the consumer. Instead, the best customers of big banks (those customers using multiple products) actually get treated the worst as in most cases they are forced to deal with different digital experiences for each product and typically have a disconnected experience between the physical branches and the digital channels.

The customer demand for banks to create an omni-channel experience is already here, particularly around products like mortgages, a traditionally bank branch driven model that's ripe for digital transformation. However, few traditional banks are showing real movement in that direction. Customers routinely use the Internet to search for interest rates and to apply for loans and credit cards. Customers are demanding that banks come to them, but many traditional banks are reluctant to do so, which is leaving them vulnerable to competition by other business models such as Quicken Loans, who are more proactive, digital, and customer centric.[1]

Social media provides the forum to drive customers to explore to alternative and more digital, customer-centric financial services. As

---

[1] http://www.pwc.com/us/en/financial-services/publications/viewpoints/assets/viewpoint-retail-bank-customer-centric-business-model.pdf

a result of this evolution, bank customers can now share their great experience with non-bank financial solutions or bad experience with their traditional bank to an average number of "150–200 friends" in a matter of minutes. Banks with outdated digital capabilities and poor service have nowhere to hide. In a study by PwC bank, 42 percent of their customers stated the number one thing they would like to see change was "Better and more personal service." An Accenture survey results suggest that banks are at a digital tipping point where they will lose customers, if they can't deliver the services customers are demanding.

Consumers are already going to alternative financial providers, sometimes referred to as "non-banks," for better products and services. In fact, the majority of consumers Accenture's survey said they went to other sources to purchase auto loans (70 percent), brokerage accounts (61 percent), registered retirement accounts (53 percent), financial advice (52 percent), and home mortgage loans (52 percent).[2]

It's not that banks aren't aware of their customers needs, touchpoints, or demands. They are awash in relevant data, but either they don't know what to do with it, are reacting too slowly, or they're ignoring it.[3]

Historical Reactive Digital Failures

Circuit City, at one time one of the largest electronics retailers in the country, went from 700-plus stores and $12 billion in revenues in the 80s to busted and bankrupt by 2009. Why? They reacted with too little, too late. According to founder Alan Wurtzel, the company used the same business strategies in 2000 as they did in 1980. If the

---

[2] http://www.forbes.com/sites/tomgroenfeldt/2015/05/11/financial-services-customers-are-fed-up/

[3] http://www.forbes.com/sites/tomgroenfeldt/2015/05/11/financial-services-customers-are-fed-up/

company had "woken up sooner," he told a *Wall Street Journal* writer,[4] they might not have crashed and burned. Wurtzel stepped down from his company in 2000 and sold his stock in it because he no longer believed in Circuit City's future.

Wurtzel said, once management finally came up with a plan, (reactive digital) they failed to execute it for one of the same reasons we see in other companies—the investments in a digital transformation that would have moved Circuit City's business forward also would have threatened its stock price.[5]

Another classic example of reactive digital was the battle for the rental DVDs and streaming media that played out between Blockbuster Video and Netflix. Blockbuster dominated the market until a new CEO cut their digital strategy and business model to adopt a brick and mortar approach. That was the point where Netflix took over and ultimately destroyed Blockbuster. Blockbuster tried to rally—reactive digital—but it was too late. Last year the last Blockbuster store closed, and Netflix is now the industry leader, fending off other digital attacks from Redbox and other disrupters.

Companies that are not digital on the inside will have difficulty being digital on the outside, resulting more in a reactive culture than a transformative one. Additionally, companies that have employees who are digitally savvy often don't take advantage of those skill sets. Therefore, their employees are unable to bring their digital intelligence inside. As a result, these companies become *reactive* rather than *proactive*. They respond digitally only when they see competitors advancing in the marketplace with digital strategies. They haven't created the organizational structures, strategies, or processes to run successful digital campaigns.

Companies worried about the bottom line cost of being transformative don't typically understand that it costs more to react and fix a problem after the fact than to prevent it from happening in the first place.

---

[4] http://blogs.wsj.com/bankruptcy/2012/10/25/lessons-from-the-death-of-circuit-city/

[5] http://blogs.wsj.com/bankruptcy/2012/10/25/lessons-from-the-death-of-circuit-city/

Defining Transformative Digital

Digital transformation is not just using an agency to redesign your website or create a new mobile app. Digital transformation is not just assigning a committee, a specialized team, or a particular employee to "monitor technology trends." It's not just being on social networks. Get the point?

Digital transformation is how a company changes their business model, customer experiences and operational processes to adapt to the way customers into today's digital age want to find, explore, buy, and interact with their goods and services.

Research shows that the majority of companies think they're engaged in a digital transformation, when only one in four actually are. A recent study reveals that 25 percent or less of companies surveyed understand what a digital touchpoint or digital transformation is, yet 88 percent of those companies confidently claim they are in the midst of a digital transformation.[6]

In other words, most of the people who claimed their companies were undergoing a digital transformation didn't even know what a digital transformation was. Many companies mistake a "redesign" of their website as a digital transformation.

A great metaphor for the difference between a redesign and a transformation is like updating an old house. Will you refurbish, redesign it, renovate, or recreate it? Redesigning a home versus renovating it is the difference between hiring a designer versus hiring an architect and an engineer.

Netflix pulled together cloud architecture, mobile apps, streaming media, and other digital capabilities to drive rapid product development across multiple teams very successfully. Jf they relied on

---

[6] http://www.forbes.com/fdc/welcome_mjx.shtml

traditional processes, procedures, and architectures, it would have only slowed them down.[7]

At the heart of digital transformation is this one immutable fact: if what you're doing isn't solving a true consumer problem or pain point, it doesn't matter what you create, or what technology you use to create it. There are no amount of bells, whistles, flash, brilliant copywriting, or technology that will entice the consumer to stay with you over the long run if you aren't solving their problems. It takes transformative digital, not reactive digital, to do that.

Ultimately, digital transformation is connecting with your customers, clients or constituents, and how they engage with your company. It's not just about apps, nor about new websites, smartphones, or computers. Technology is what enables you to create those connections and automate operations and processes, but technology in and of itself is not the goal or the heart of digital transformation. Technology is simply the vehicle that drives your company brand and model into the hearts, souls, and minds of your customers.

A truly transformative digital model also transforms how a company achieves authentic customer connections. Additionally, your business model(s) depends on what product or services you're offering. Chances are once these models are pointed out to you, you'll recognize them and how they work. Take for instance an "on-demand" business model such as Amazon's Prime Now or InstaCart. These on-demand models generate revenue from people who want or need to have something right away. People are also willing to pay more for a product or service they can have right away. Their time is more valuable than money.

Customers want a cheaper, faster, better, and more engaging experience with the companies they do business with. They want an immediate customer experience that can be facilitated from a smartphone,

---

[7] http://www.forbes.com/sites/jasonbloomberg/2014/07/23/agile-enterprise -architecture-finally-crosses-the-chasm/2/

a computer, tablet, or handheld device. Whether they're ordering food, buying music, books, mattresses, eyeglasses, or apparel, they want a simple, seamless, easy way to do it. Digital transformation is about *reimagining* and then *recreating* the customer experience.

A transformative digital business model will incorporate cloud technology architecture to platform the business, leverage big data to make decisions, be mobile centric, and incorporate social media to engage customers. It's that realignment of business models that presents the greatest challenge to most companies.

Study after study shows digitally mature companies far outperform their non-digital competitors. Forbes and the MIT Center for Digital Business examined more than 400 large mainstream companies around the globe. They found that digital leaders enjoy a significant advantage over their non-digital competitors. Their analysis also found that digital companies are 26 percent more profitable than their average industry competitors and enjoy a 12 percent higher market valuation. Additionally, digital companies generate 9 percent more revenue with their existing physical capacity and drive more efficiency in their existing products and processes.[8] Implementing a digital transformation isn't about whether or not to get on the latest, greatest bandwagon—it's about becoming a more profitable, more valuable business.

While digital transformation is an iterative journey where the end of one leg of the journey is really the beginning of another.

Traits of Transformative Companies

What does it take to be a company that has a real shot at transforming itself? There are many standout traits we have seen that repeat themselves after years working with enterprises around the world and not surprisingly, over time the same traits of companies that are successful in making change occur, emerge over and over again.

---

[8] http://www.forbes.com/sites/ciocentral/2013/03/10/the-dna-of-digital-leaders/

To start with, companies that are able to evolve are always in a mode of planning for both the long and short term. Integrated into their ongoing planning is the consideration of big and small data, which they factor into their decisions. They never consider this data in a vacuum, instead accumulating context along with the data they're collecting. They literally look at the things around something to better understand the thing itself. Data rarely makes sense and is of little use to strategic thinkers if it is not presented with context. In an obvious case, the data may tell you that the majority of your customers buying rain gear are in Washington state, but the context tells you that not only does it rain more in Washington State, there are more communities of people engaging in the outdoors via running, biking, hiking, fishing, and kayaking. The more you accumulate context, the more you understand your customers.

Most companies *think* they put people first, but in reality they're more focused on products, services, and profits. Transformative companies focus on people and are concerned with how to better engage them. When an organization stays focused on people, they naturally care to listen to their customers. They understand that servicing their customer well leads to long-term engagement. In addition, they learn that the *way* their customers act in specific circumstances translates into very powerful data. Understanding *why* they act in those ways is the context and the key to more effective and profound digital transformation.

Transformative companies are lead by people that look for and study trends and practice trend analysis—a way of looking at information in an attempt to predict future events. By accurately predicting future trends, such as people moving from a desktop environment to a mobile one (smartphones and tablets), companies can move to meet an anticipated demand before it happens.

Culturally speaking, these types of companies almost always invest in and encourage innovation, even during hard times. They recognize that failure is part of the innovation process and they encourage both, acknowledging that success is founded upon failure. To be effective at innovation, they work closely with technical and marketing staff to determine marketing opportunities that may be opening up as a result of studying trends and context and data.

Perhaps transactional but no less important, transformative companies we work with know how to create prototypes. They recognize that prototypes don't have to be perfect and are part of a process, not the end result. They know prototypes are designed to give the company and the beta testers and designers something to gauge an idea or a concept. This also connects them back to their people (customer and employees) who become part of the process of determining what direction new products and services will take over time.

Last, companies that are successful at change hire and reward great leadership, and denounce politicking and bureaucracy. This means taking risks, making certain decisions quickly, and not requiring every move to be approved by a committee or onerous governance process. This type of leadership almost always comes from the top down, and requires leadership by example.

Companies That Are Disrupting
Case Study: Uber

The ecosystem around Uber involved massive delays, costs, and expensive barriers to become a taxi-cab driver. Cities and municipalities limited the number of drivers they would license, thus creating a shortage and driving up the cost of a cab ride for consumers. There were inflated prices and lousy service because taxis or private limos were the only game in town. The use of dispatchers and the whole cabbie culture also created extra costs which ultimately got passed down to us, the consumer.

Uber changed all that. Their unique business model transformed the system. Yes, they build a great mobile app, but it was the business model that leveraged existing technology that turned the industry on its head. Uber bypassed the dispatcher, the costs, and the ugly yellow cars. Instead they put riders in cars without all the hassles, costs, and barriers a taxi would. So if you live in a rural area where there's not likely to be a taxi company (too expensive), chances are very high there's an Uber driver.

Did Uber drive that digital transformation? No. Customers looking for a better ride did. And that brings us to the most important message of this book. Digital transformation doesn't follow a change in your business strategy. It *is* the total business strategy that transforms your business model.

When a "cease and desist" protest against UberPop—the French local ride-sharing equivalent of UberX in the United States—didn't work, French police arrested two of the company's executives. The men will face charges based on carrying out "deceptive commercial practices," permitting "illegal taxi services" and "illicit storage of personal data." The charges come amid mounting pressure on French authorities to curb what critics have called unfair, anticompetitive practices by Uber. Mass protests have hit major cities across France, and in the United States, with local taxi drivers accusing authorities of creating one rule for them and another for Uber. Authorities around the world aren't sure how to react yet.

History has also shown that while you might be able to legislate and regulate business, regulation can't ultimately prevent inevitable innovation. We see that from when Great Britain tried to legislate distribution of technology during the Industrial Revolution and failed miserably. While taxi drivers are demanding regulation to stop Uber they'll find out, as many companies do, regulation can't stop undeniable customer demand. In fact, Larry Downes and Paul Nunes, authors of the book, *Big Bang Disruption*, said "regulators will be left unable to justify limits that no longer have economic, social or political rationales. The devastation when it comes will be that much more dramatic."

Case Study: Warby Parker

Warby Parker founders weren't career eyewear specials. They were students that sparked the idea from a hiking trip where one of them lost his glasses. When he went to replace them, they were so expensive that he started grad school without them and squinted for an entire semester. They discovered the entire industry is dominated by a monopoly.

The founders said they had two goals: (1) offer an alternative to the overpriced and underwhelming eyewear that was available to us, and (2) build a business that could solve problems instead of creating them.

What Warby Parker did was look at a problem that everyone has. If you wear eyeglasses, which many people do, why does it cost $400 or more for a pair of prescription eyeglasses? How is that reasonable? Why should that be?

Warby Parker quickly figured out that prescription eyeglass prices were exorbitant because the supply chain is old and complex and too many people have their hands in the pie. So they created a disruptive digital business that sells glasses.

They design, buy, and manufacture them very inexpensively overseas. Yet, they're still very high quality. The reality is, it's very cheap to make quality eyeglass frames. For example, if you spend $300 on a pair of designer sunglasses, you might be freaked out to know that they're actually made in China for $1.50. It's the supply chain, though, that eats away at all the profit. So, they designed their own frames, then they created their own manufacturing process and started to sell directly to consumers.

What is the disruptive business model and where does digital transformation come in? They used digital to transact all of their business. They created a web-based version of software that lets consumers try on glasses virtually in an effective manner. So, Warby Parker will sell you prescription eyeglasses that are very beautiful, very well made, very design conscious, and very (compared to the average shop) inexpensive. Instead of going where you used to buy eyeglasses and paying $450, you can get four pairs for the price of one at Warby Parker. Do you see how that site is very disruptive to all kinds of traditional eyeglass companies? That is digital transformation at its core.

Case Study: Casper.com

Casper Sleep is doing to mattresses what Warby Parker did to eyeglasses. Did you ever wonder why a decent mattress for your home costs over $1,000? Even if you're willing and able to spend that much money, are you really happy about the average mattress shopping experience? A new website wasn't the solution—a new business model and way of delivering the product being sold through the website was the solution.

Like Warby Parker, Casper Sleep went in search of a solution to a specific problem. They eliminated the need for showrooms and are selling mattresses direct online. They now offer a zero-risk, 100-night trial of any of their mattresses. If your mattress isn't perfect for any reason, they'll send a courier to pick up the mattress and refund you 100 percent of the price. They are able to do away with the need for a showroom because they figured out a way to compress a mattress into a package size that could be shipped through normal delivery channels. This enabled them to lower the cost of delivery and simplify the trial experience.

The examples above are designed to get you thinking, "Where do I go from here?" or even better, "I have to be even more prepared to preemptively strike against this disruption than I realized. Because if I thought I was safe in my industry, I'm wrong." The truth is that no industry is safe; change is coming.

What if you could apply similar transformative business principles that companies like Google, Amazon, Apple, and other companies riding the digital transformation wave have? Imagine if MetLife, for instance, could change the way insurance is bought in the way that Apple changed the way computers and gadgets were sold?

Traditional Companies That Are Transforming

Some of the best, largest, and most well-known companies that have digitally transformed themselves include Nike, Disney, and Burberry.

Case Study: Burberry

"I grew up in a physical world, and I speak English. The next generation is growing up in a digital world, and they speak social."

—Angela Ahrendts, CEO of Burberry

Somewhere along the line Burberry, the most famous Trench coat manufacturer of all, forgot the iconic coat their company was founded on.

When Angela Ahrendts became CEO of Burberry in 2006, the first thing she asked was, "Where are the trench coats?" More than 60 managers had braved the cold, damp weather to be at their first strategic meeting, yet not one of them was wearing the iconic coat the company was known for. Additionally, offshore manufacturing and other business practices had compromised the brand to the point Burberry had lost its former luxury reputation.

Ahrendts promptly spent the next 6 months traveling the globe to gauge the extent of the damage to the brand before changing the company's business model and committing to a digital transformation. Using technology, she created videos for salespeople to use to explain why the Burberry Trenchcoats were so expensive ($1,500 and up), and gave salespeople iPads and stores audiovisual equipment so they could "tell the Burberry story."

Her use of technology didn't stop with iPads. Ahrendts also created new websites, and had the company rethink their entire marketing approach, making it digital. She consolidated all the regional websites and redesigned everything on one platform to showcase every facet of the brand. The new website became the hub of the company's marketing and branding. Now the iconic Burberry Trench-coat is the first thing customers see when they go online. Burberry launched theartofthetrench.com in 2009, showing off photos of celeb-rities and historical figures wearing their Trenchcoat and encouraging customers to submit photos of themselves in their own coats.

They recently began to offer customization of the Trenchcoat online, offering some 12 million possible styles. While it's taken years to transform the company, it's happened, and all around a vision of returning to the company's iconic roots. The transformation paid off. Today 60 percent of Burberry's business is apparel, and outerwear makes up more than half of that. At the end of fiscal 2012, Burberry's revenues and operating income had doubled over the previous 5 years, to $3 billion and $600 million, respectively.[9]

The website, the stores, the brand are all designed to speak to that millennial consumer through emotive Burberry brand content: music, movies, heritage, storytelling. "More people visit our platform every week than walk into all our stores combined," Ahrendt says.[10]

Takeaways from Burberry:

- Stick with your core product and stand by your vision. There will always be critics. Once you understand your core product, have your vision and set your goals, trust yourself to reach them.

- Share, engage, and involve your customers, your employees, and even your critics. Make sure people understand your vision as much as is possible, but don't let their lack of understanding derail you.

---

[9] https://hbr.org/2013/01/burberrys-ceo-on-turning-an-aging-british-icon-into-a-global-luxury-brand

[10] https://hbr.org/2013/01/burberrys-ceo-on-turning-an-aging-british-icon-into-a-global-luxury-brand

- If you lose your focus, you can regain it. It doesn't matter whether you, or the person in charge before you, lost the company's focus; it can be regained. Organizations that focus on the competition rather than their own strengths tend to lose focus.

Case Study: Disney

"The riskiest thing you may do is maintain the status quo."

—Bob Iger, CEO and CDO of Disney

At Disney the CEO is the Chief Transformation Officer (CTO), that's how important digital, and the customer experience is to Disney. Disney was an innovator from the beginning. They have always focused on the customer experience—perhaps more than any other company in the world. What many people don't know about Disney is that they drive their phenomenal success with their strong commitment to new technology, gathering, analyzing, and using data to enhance the consumer experience.

Disney recently invested $1 billion investment in the "MyMagic+" band. The new band, Disney says, serves as "a multi-channel, multi-platform digital experience initiative." The band, the website, and a mobile application all allow visitors to customize their visit in different ways. The wristbands also serve as a guest's park ticket, room key, FastPass ride ticket, PhotoPass, and means of purchasing food and other products on property. Guests can preplan the day's Fast Passes and making dinner reservations in one place. Not only does the band make visitor's time in the magic kingdom easier, it provides even more data Disney can use to continue to enhance the user experience the next time they visit.

Data Disney collects also helps them manage their staff. Labor costs account for almost half of the expenses at the park. Being able to track demand and schedule employees gives Disney control over every aspect of both the customer and the visitor experience.

Physical age doesn't matter at Disney, but mental age does. You might be surprised to know that the biggest thought leaders, CEOs, and experts on digital transformation were also board members for Disney. Jack Dorsey, co-founder of Twitter and CEO and co-founder of Square; Sheryl Sandberg, COO of Facebook; the late Steve Jobs, former CEO of Apple; Orin Smith, former CEO of Starbucks.

Takeaways from Disney:

- The future is digital so your employees, officers, board, and management should not only understand it, but embrace it. If they don't, you need to hire people who do.

- Trendwatching is critical. Not only does it enable you to spot patterns and trends before they become mainstream, but it's a rich source of inspiration, creativity, and innovation.

- When your business model is *the experience*, invest in, and focus heavily on data analytics to ensure that your customers are having the best experience possible.

Case Study: Nike

"We have been on this for a long time. We didn't just wake up one day and say that this digital thing seemed interesting."

—Stefan Olander, Vice-President of Nike's Digital Sport

Nike, the world's leading innovator of athletic footwear, apparel, and accessories, built its company around innovations. When digital technologies began to emerge in the 1990s, Nike was quick to explore the possibilities. From letting customers order customized colored sneakers online, to creating a community of like-minded weekend warriors or extreme athletes, Nike reaped significant business benefits from digital.

When social media, the Internet, and the technology came along, Nike was waiting. They embraced digital like it was a long lost family member. Because they've always focused on people who purchased their products, their only goal has always been to "connect with athletes to inspire and enable them to be better." That consumer engagement mindset is probably best understood by their recent (2014) decision to discontinue one of their most popular technologies—the Fuelband and the Nike+ Training App.

A testament to their focus on the consumer to the exclusion of product and revenue is the Nike Fuelband, an activity tracker worn on the wrist. The band allows users to track their physical activity, including how many steps they've taken daily, and how much energy or calories they've burned throughout the day.

Data from the Fuelband is integrated into the Nike+ online community. Wearers cannot only monitor their progress and achievements, they can share that data with friends on social media, or compete with others for points and awards. When it was released in 2012, the Fuelband was wildly successful, even though a University of Pennsylvania study showed of all the fitness wearables, it was the least accurate. The Nike fan base drove the popularity of the device and would still be driving it, if Nike hadn't opted to discontinue the band in 2014. The reason? In a market rapidly becoming saturated with fitness wearables, almost all of whom were more accurate than the Fuelband, Nike concluded it no longer needed to manufacture its own gadget.

Measuring, sharing, and incorporating performance into the customer lifestyle was, and still is a big part of Nike digital, but not at the expense of the customer experience. By focusing on deepening their connection with their customers, and not on making a better wearable, they both personalized and amplified their "Just Do It," slogan. That's how Nike captures their customers' hearts, not just their wallets.

Takeaways from Nike:

- **It's okay to let go of a disruptive product even if others are pursuing it.** When Nike stepped away from its Fuelband, they did so because they recognized it was the software and applications, not the physical product, that created the customer interaction and engagement they sought.

- **Understand what business you're truly in and stick to it.**
There was no fitness wearable when the Fuelband was released
in 2012. In less than 3 years, however, the market was all but
saturated. Nike watched the market, realized there was competition from better performing wearable products and stuck
to its original goal—to "connect with athletes to inspire and
enable them to be better." Nike understood when it came to
producing wearables it was in the software business and Apple
was in the hardware business. They made appropriate digital
decisions to partner with companies who were in the hardware
business.

- **Great digital companies remain focused on engaging
with their consumers.** They aren't swayed with emerging
technologies unless those technologies can help them improve
or maintain that engagement.

- **Capture the consumers' hearts, not just their wallets.**
Never forget that people, not technology, drive true digital
transformation.

Case Study: UPS

Sometimes changes even extended into other areas, such as the
way you do training. For example, at United Parcel Service (UPS)
drivers make an average of 100 deliveries a day, often under adverse
conditions in bad weather. It's no surprise new drivers may experienced a high slip and fall rate during their first year on the job. Those
slips, trips, and falls could cost UPS billions of dollars a year in lost
time, workers compensation, and replacement employee costs. Like
many companies, UPS used PowerPoint presentations and lectures to
train their drivers about slip and fall risks and about how not to slip.
When they learned that wasn't working, they didn't just add more
classes and more PowerPoint presentations. They radically changed
the way they educated their drivers about slips and falls.

UPS got a government grant and went to Virginia Tech's Department of Industrial and Systems Engineering department and professor Thurmon Lockhart. Working with Professor Lockhart, they came up with a radical solution—retrain the brain kinesthetically. They developed a slip-and-fall simulator that allowed UPS drivers to actually experience slips, trips, and falls in real time, on real surfaces. Drivers were suspended by a harness system that kept them from getting hurt, but their brains and bodies experienced the sensation of an actual fall and learned to compensate for it, making drivers safer on various types of surfaces.

The simulator was very effective. After a series of successful training outcomes and requests for simulators, a new company was born. Several Virginia tech alumni engineers started Industrial Biodynamics around manufacturing the simulator. Now UPS sends all their drivers for the 30-minute hands-on training on one of the two simulators they now own.

Several companies in a variety of industries, including manufacturing, healthcare, and even law enforcement and crews at Los Alamos National Security Center use or have trained on the simulators. UPS may have transformed their training, but Industrial Biodynamics is transforming the slip and fall industry.[11]

If transformation is so profitable, then why aren't more companies doing it? Chapter 3 focuses on exactly the reasons why.

---

[11] https://www.vt.edu/spotlight/impact/2010-01-04-falls/fall-prevention.html

3

Why Traditional Companies
Are Failing at Digital

Companies fail at digital every day for a variety of reasons and they suddenly find their business is taking a beating and their competitors have passed them by while they're sitting there and wondering, "What happened?" This may be because the company's leadership or designated digital team is not monitoring what's happening around them. Sometimes they casually observe what's happening, but they have no process in place to contextualize and measure what they're seeing. It may be their culture, their IT department, their inability to spot, or follow trends. Whatever the reason, they're failing. We will cover the most common reasons in this chapter, but first let's start with an example.

Two of the biggest, most well-documented and talked about digital transformation failures are Borders and Barnes & Noble. The winner in the bookstore battle was, of course, Amazon—who never intended to be just a bookstore at all. In a speech to the American Association of Booksellers in 1999, Amazon founder, Jeff Bezos said, "We don't view ourselves as a bookstore or a music store. We want to be the place for someone to find and discover everything they want to buy."

Bezos started Amazon by creating a list of 20 potential products he thought might sell well via the Internet, including software, CDs, books, office supplies, and apparel. Because of the sheer number of

SKUs in the millions, and the fact that books sold in one store were the same as books sold in another store, books became his first, and most obvious choice of product. No physical bookstore could stock millions of titles, but a "virtual" bookstore could. After books came DVDs and CDs. Amazon.com opened its virtual doors in July 1995. By September 1996, the company had 100 employees and more than $15.7 million in sales.

Amazon's success didn't go unnoticed by Barnes & Noble, who countered with their own website, and a claim that readers could access more books than they could on Amazon. But by then Amazon was also selling CDs and DVDs. They had become much more than a bookstore, adding toys, music, movies, gifts, electronics and more to their site, but it was content that made them grow, and the Kindle that made them king.

Kindle went to market 4 years after Barnes & Noble had stopped selling ebooks entirely.[1] It wasn't the first ereader on the market, but it was the best. Why? Because Jeff Bezos waited 7 years for reader technology to advance enough for the Kindle to bypass the issues his predecessors experienced.

The first Kindle represented the kind of technology that would launch the digital transformation that would create a new kind of relationship with the mobile consumer. The Kindle did for content what the smartphone did for apps—it opened a million markets and provided untold opportunities to change the media industry. Amazon didn't want to sell books as much as they wanted to own the content consumption platform with a device as desirable as a smartphone.

While turning out a new, better and more improved version of the Kindle almost every 18 months, Amazon announced that "Prime" subscribers to Amazon.com would also get free access to almost 3,000

---

[1] http://goodereader.com/blog/electronic-readers/a-brief-history-of-ebooks

Fox TV shows and movies. Prime subscribers could also get free access to a Kindle *e-book library*. So, now, for about the cost of 10 paperbacks, you get free shipping, thousands of television shows and movies, and a library where you can check out up to 10 books and keep them as long as you like. As of this writing there are over 3.6 million books in the Kindle library, and more than 40 million Amazon Prime members.

By offering more incentives and reasons for consumers to download content rather than order it delivered, Amazon cut down on the number of physical orders it had to fulfill. Using that same thought process, they cut a deal with Fox TV to stream or download shows and movies. Every television series or season of shows watched online, or on a Kindle Fire, was another heavy-box set that didn't have to be processed, packaged, and shipped. Not only was Amazon saving money on employees who had to retrieve, prep, pack, and ship the product, they saved millions on postage and shipping costs. Amazon was a huge success, but had Barnes & Noble acted quicker they may have stopped Amazon in its rush to become the superstore it is today.

Amazon only sold books when it launched. That was the point where had Barnes & Noble acted differently they could have prevented Amazon's bookselling growth. Yet Barnes & Noble, like many traditional companies of that era, failed to focus on digital.

To take a page from Stephen Covey's time management quadrant, too many companies are watching the urgent things, not the important ones. Urgent things demand immediate attention and are often associated with the achievement of someone else's goals. Important matters have an outcome that leads to the achievement of your goals. The secret to effective digital transformation is a lot like effective time management—focus on the important before it becomes the urgent.

When companies fail to pay attention to emerging opportunities, their competitors not only trounce them, they gain the extra capital to move in and grow even bigger.

Barnes & Noble's customers wanted to order items online and pick them up in the store in their neighborhood, or they wanted to be in the store and say, "Oh you don't have this," and then order it right in the store from barnesandnoble.com and have it shipped to their house. They have that capability now, and they've probably had it for 5 years or more. But they didn't have it when it counted. They failed digitally when they didn't make that move and they let Amazon continue to grow its customer base and build loyalty.

It's not to say that Amazon wouldn't have existed, but they may not have gained the dominance they did through online books had Barnes & Noble acted differently.

Transformation is not looking at who you think your competitors are, or looking at who you think your digital native competitors are; so you can copycat them. You have to figure out what is unique to your business and find leverage that others can't.

Barnes & Noble's strategic advantage was their superior real estate assets and great brand name. Barnes & Noble had the footprint, and it had the operations and it had all the right things going for it, but they weren't paying attention. At the time people were ordering books on Amazon, but there were a lot of people who were saying, "I still like my neighborhood Barnes & Noble store. I like the feel of a book and I like to sit down in the Starbucks in the Barnes & Noble and enjoy those big puffy chairs while I read my book."

What occurred between Amazon and Barnes & Noble is happening across many industries today. For example, connected car technology (your automobile having a permanent connection to the Internet) is already going mainstream. Who is paying attention? Not many. Companies are saying, "It'll never happen." Those are famous last words of too many failed companies.

Connected cars may not be mainstream next year, or even 5 years from now, but if I'm a Ford executive, I better be building that car and spending money experimenting with it to see if I can figure out exactly where it's going and how my customers are going to want that experience.

If you're a company of any size, you don't want to wait until an idea or concept is accepted before taking action. Companies fail to transform for many reasons, primarily because executives don't take the time or don't know how to look out for the signs as to where the trends are taking their business. But there are dozens of other reasons companies fail at digital. Here's the list:

Business Reasons Companies Fail at Digital

Not Capitalizing on Unique Differentiators

Instead of treating trends as something that could materialize into opportunities for them, they say, "It's never going to be anything serious," and act accordingly, turning their attention away from opportunities that begin to pop up almost too fast to take advantage of.

They need to realize that many of these trends will indeed happen or that certain distinct trends, when combined down the line, will bring about great change. For example, the smartphone required the convergence of touch screens, high speed mobile data service, and extended battery life provided by lithium technology. Any of those technologies on their own may have not gotten industry leaders to pay attention.

The logical next step to take after spotting a trend is not to ask "will it happen?" but to ask, "how long will it take for these trends to manifest in my target market and how can we prepare to get there ahead of our competitors?"

Having Digital Tactics without Digital Vision

So many companies have missed opportunities around digital transformation because the company's executives didn't have the ability to look down the road 10 or 15 years and envision how digital will evolve. They fail because they can't figure out what is unique to their business that they can exploit that others can't and then drive a wedge into that.

There are far too many billion dollar companies where CEOs have ignored trends, calling them fads. They made limited vision assumptions such as assuming that people will listen to music just downloads because bandwidth would never support good audio quality. Meanwhile digital leaders like Apple, were sitting back and waiting for the bandwidth to catch up, and allow better quality, the companies who had a chance at the opportunity of the century were missing the boat.

To be competitive, companies should envision where things are going in their industry as well as other industries and get real about potential new product and service creations of the future. They should lead in their space, not follow.

3D printing is an example of an emerging technology poised to significantly impact several industries including manufacturing, packaging, and transportation. Traditional businesses like Staples and Home Depot recently launched print-on-premises plans. Anyone with a thumb-drive can stop into one of their stores and have an item quickly printed for them using the store's 3D printer. Amazon also saw the potential—launching a 3D printing store where customers can shop for and order products that can be printed and shipped on demand.[2]

Comparing Oneself to Competitors Only and Not Best Practices

The prime example of this is GPS manufacturers. While TomTom, Magellan, and Garmin were making better, and more expensive, GPS devices, Apple invented the smartphone. Then someone else invented the free GPS iPhone app. The best ideas, and often the most troublesome to your industry, may be found outside of your industry.

Put your research findings into context. Often we see companies failing at their own industries because they are only focusing on their competitors and not on best practices across other industries. It's rare

---

[2] http://www.amazon.com/b?node=8323871011

that your competitors are far enough ahead to provide the kind of best practices that can stimulate your industry.

Lack of Focus on Ongoing Customer and Client Engagement versus Just Sales

If you learn anything from Blockbuster being taken out by Netflix, it should be that you've got to invest in digital. You may need to meter your investment so you'll last until it's truly mainstream, but at least you'll be there first, you'll be ahead of the curve because you've been experimenting along the way. You'll have learned things later adopters won't know, and you'll be a leader in that space, not a follower.

Remember how Barnes & Noble's failure to recognize the "omnichannel experience"—how they dropped the ebook reader, embraced short sightedness . . . and didn't run with a fully mobile ecommerce site. That's how they helped open the doors to Amazon's spectacular growth.

How big was Barnes & Noble's failure? Well, Morgan Stanley estimates that Amazon sold $3.57 billion worth of Kindle ereaders and tablets in 2012, $4.5 billion in Kindle device sales in 2013 and $5 billion in Kindle device sales in 2014.[3] This is not just a measure of their product sales success, it's a measure of customer engagement as well. The kindle is a content distribution system, and the average reader of all ages was clearly buying into the concept. This allowed amazon to engage its customers consistently, and sell them content that was substitute for printed books and magazines.

Whether a company crashes and burns, or crashes and ultimately succeeds, their failures provide rich case studies for the rest of us about what *not to* do and what *to* do. By studying the failures around you, you can see where things might have gone right, and where they

---

[3] http://allthingsd.com/20130812/amazon-to-sell-4-5-billion-worth-of-kindles-this-year-morgan-stanley-says/?mod=obinsite

definitely went wrong. If you don't study where others have failed, chances are you'll follow in their footsteps.

Marketplace Reasons Companies Fail at Digital

Customer Base Has Become More Digitally Sophisticated That Perceived

Companies, particularly brick and mortar companies, get comfortable with their older, non-digital customers. They slow down their digital journey and delay or stop changing. They don't understand the digital shift will happen when people start interacting with the new model. Kodak failed to see people giving up film for the convenience and less expensive alternative of digital.

Circuit City continued to resist digital until it was too late and too expensive to even react digitally, let alone transform. Best Buy, their closest competitor, heard the wakeup call Circuit City ignored. Best Buy launched a massive internal effort to educate its employees about digital transformation, even creating a "customer-centricity university" for their employees. They changed their business model and their strategy and senior leadership at Best Buy saw to it that the entire organization embraced a customer-centric approach.

Blockbuster failed to see customers moving toward streaming content. Companies like those we just mentioned fail to understand their customer base and move to meet it. For example, we both have mothers who now love their Kindles. They made the change from paperbacks to ebooks. However, they still prefer to go call the airline to book their flights because booking a flight online isn't as easy a shift as a Kindle.

What we see is that some people acclimate toward some online changes, but not others. It's a sign of a changing customer base and their comfort or discomfort with digital. When a change happens, as changes always do, people like our moms, who are digital immigrants who weren't raised with technology, can't adapt to the changes. In other words, people from an older generation, or an ethnic generation who don't have the backgrounds in technology often have significant trouble adapting. They may be able to adapt in one area but unable to cross over into other technology areas.

Many companies see their currently non-digital customers who prefer a physical connection to a digital one, as a reason not to transform. Blockbuster made this mistake, switching from digital back to the concept of a physical store, a "7–11 convenience store" concept where families drove to their nearest Blockbuster, and wandered for hours around the store physically shifting through a limited selection of movies.

Blockbuster failed to realize or acknowledge that customers were moving away from their stores, preferring the convenience of ordering DVDs online rather than going to a store with a limited selection, and many current releases often out of stock. Customers also didn't like the late fees, a $400 million bonus in Blockbuster's coffers, but a strong irritant for customers who had to remember to return the DVD to the store on time or be charged late fees. Blockbuster also allowed customers to swap out some DVDs for others for no charge, but then later limited the numbers of DVDs they could do that with.

Lack of Focus on Creating Streamlined Intuitive Customer Experience

Just as restaurants go out of their way to make their customer experience easy, pleasant, and simple, the digital experience should do the same. When companies don't understand the customer experience and each touchpoint along the way, they fail at digital.

For instance, seniors are now "facetiming" their grandchildren, finding the best travel deals on Kayak, or paying bills online. They're still digital immigrants, sometimes struggling with the Internet, or certain apps or websites, but many times they struggle because the company they want to do business with makes it difficult to interact or engage in a streamlined, effective way.

Creating the best customer experience means collecting data about how your customers find you, how they explore your company, make buying decisions, how they prefer to purchase and where and how they give you feedback, among other things. Not understanding each one of these touchpoints and creating and implementing a business model, strategy, and processes to address them is yet another reason why companies fail.

Lack of Understanding of How Digital Has Changed Desire for Ownership versus Sharing Economy

In order for a sharing economy model to work, both the consumer and the company have to be trustworthy and trust each other. That's a radical departure for the traditional business model, but a crucial prerequisite for this particular model.

"The power behind the sharing economy," says Rachel Botsman, author of *What's Mine Is Yours*, a book on the sharing economy, "is using the power of technology to build trust among strangers."

Just because this sometimes touchy-feely business model has a "sit-around-the-campfire-and-sing-Kumbaya," feel to it, don't think of the sharing economy as a warm, quaint, but passing fad. Botsman says the consumer peer-to-peer rental market alone is worth $26 billion. That's a lot of trust and a powerful economy. Companies who fail at digital fail to see how to tap into a socioeconomic ecosystem of human and physical resources.

Lack of Ability to Quickly Adapt to Trends

Companies fail because they throw away first-mover advantage by not having a strategy. One of the messages for the traditional companies in these days when things are moving so quickly, and information is doubling every 12 months is to have a plan in place for when technology and trends do intersect.

Organizational Reasons Companies Fail at Digital

No Digital Leader with Decision Autonomy, Direct Budget, or P&L Responsibility

Companies may have many individuals throughout the company who have digital titles, but no power to implement or control digital change.

You need to appoint a Chief Digital Officer, and not just in name. The position must come with a realistic budget, power, and the authority to act and someone else overseeing whether that budget is being spent wisely. Blockbuster had a CEO committed to digital transformation, then fired him and hired a CEO with absolutely no interest in digital. Without anyone to champion, implement. and push digital, it took less than 18 months for Blockbuster to lose ground to Netflix.

C-Suite and Leadership Not Involved in Company's Digital Strategy

They also fail to prepare employees for changes in working in a digital culture—resulting in resistance, sabotage, or turnover. Being an innovative, forward thinking, thought leader kind of manager isn't enough to drive a successful transformation. Companies have to have everyone on board with the transformation—from the C-suite to the employees in the mail room. Buy-in from employees and management is critical.

Digital Team Is Too Top Heavy or Bottom Heavy

Companies who don't know how to staff for digital transformation and don't have the right accountability to ensure that digital is spending its budget wisely and appropriately when they do fund it, tend to fail.

Digital Not Embedded in Corporate Culture

Company culture can kill digital before it even has a chance. Existing systems can cause a company to fail at digital. People, teams, systems, policies, and procedures that are known, that are safe and understood, often fail when confronted with a companywide change. Call it resistance, or call it having to relearn, rethink, and rework "the way we've always done it," but when they don't or can't institute a digital culture, companies fail.

Trying to Do Everything 100 Percent In-House or Outsourced

Trying to effect a digital transformation entirely in house with your current staff usually results in failure. Every company needs to have internal people who understand the company, the culture, and digital. They're the ones who can deal with the day-to-day demands of the company as well as the digital processes. Equally important is hiring outside staff that live and breathe digital and can focus on just the digital transformation. Not only can they focus on digital, they almost always bring fresh perspectives to your process, model, and procedures from other industries.

They Settle on the Wrong People in Key Digital Team Roles

The people skills necessary to be part of making digital successful are really no different than the people skills necessary to make part of any organization or business successful.

You need strong leaders and genuinely strong leadership. You need people who can make decisions and execute them without too much fear. In other words, in order to do this well, you're going to be invoking change. What we know about people is that many of them fear change and a lot of them resist it because they don't understand how the changes are going to impact them. Are they going to have a job after the transformation? Do they have the job skills needed for the new incarnation of their position? Will they need more training?

You may eliminate 50 jobs in an auto plant, to create 150 different jobs somewhere else. The fact is people need to change for progress to happen. It all boils down to employees and management accepting that. Look at your own skills and those of your employees.

What kind of skills do people need to have that are running digital groups or rethinking their entire business because of digital? They need to be able to make decisions. They need to be able to lead. They need to be able to invoke change in whatever way you want to describe it.

You don't want to be frozen in fear either and end up saying, "we're not going to do it this way because no one's ever done it yet." The fact that no one has ever done it is exactly the point. No one has done it yet and you've got to step out in front of it.

You'll also need to have good managerial skills to manage teams and build a culture around digital. That is, you'll need to hire and attract people who are passionate about digital, who want to do things differently and want to take risks. In this day and age those are sound generic traits and what you need and want in any group of people that's trying to be successful at something.

Operational Reasons Companies Fail at Digital

Reliance on Traditional Heavy Processes and Reluctance to Lightweight Processes

Successful companies have developed a lot of processes and best practices. Their ability to do this is usually why they have succeeded. They fail when they assume their excellence in creating and implementing new digital processes will be more of the same, but it's not.

The truth is, nobody really understands digital processes as much as they do other processes because they are so new, and they're changing daily. Creating new processes for digital is about learning, implementing, and changing your processes as you go.

Lack of Enterprise-Wide Digital Spend Oversight

Even if you do commit to a budget, it's important to watch over it to ensure you're (1) not duplicating efforts, (2) spreading the money for digital out between multiple business units, and not optimizing your spending. For example, we have observed companies with multiple business units competing against themselves on paid search phrase bidding as the multiple business units have different relevance to the same search terms. Had they aggregating their effort, they would likely spend less and appropriately allocate the traffic.

Digital Is Controlled within Silos

Most companies operate as silos—they need to. Silos (departments, divisions, groups like sales, marketing, manufacturing, etc.) are needed to provide the structure a company needs to function. Silos are a naturally occurring part of the business structure. Information typically flows up and down, but rarely side-to-side. That's where companies fail—by failing to eliminate the problems silos cause. The goal is not to destroy or get rid of the silo. The goal is rather to eliminate the silo mentality that silo structures can often create.

A silo mentality is a mindset where certain departments, or even all departments, compete against each other in the same company. Even if they're not competing, they're not sharing information within the same company. Not only does a silo mentality reduce efficiency overall, it reduces morale, creates paranoia, cynicism, and eventually contributes to the failure of a productive culture, product, or division.

Technology Reasons Companies Fail at Digital

Legacy Infrastructure Is the Excuse for Not Transforming

Financial services organizations more than $500 billion annually on technology.[4] Banks were early adaptors of technology—and many of them still use original mainframes and infrastructure. However, it's exactly that kind and age of technology, complexity, cost, and IT issues that cause so many banks to fail at digital.

Current systems are notoriously fragmented and complex. As a result, many banks have huge problems with data quality and consistency.[5] Banks and financial institutions may have inherited their restrictions, regulations, and a system that's not easily sourced to the cloud, but too many companies can't get out of their own way even when it's affordable and doable.

Lack of Internal Use of Social Collaboration Capabilities

Today many employees are almost always younger, better, and more savvy digital natives than their digital immigrant counterparts and co-workers. They're often more on-board, more digitally active, yet more restrained by upper management who are generally older and less digitally or technically savvy. The CEOs and company officers of larger, corporate companies almost always tend to be digital immigrants, are older, and comfortable with different processes, including how they communicate. Like any immigrant they struggle with the (digital) language, the social culture, and the big picture. Rather than push past their discomfort and learn new ways, they settle in somewhere between comfort and fear and hang out there hoping it's enough. It's usually just enough to guarantee companywide failure.

---

[4] http://www.economist.com/node/15016132

[5] http://www.economist.com/node/15016132

4

Unlocking Business Opportunity in Digital Trends

The connection between digital disruption and observing digital trends is important, but it is not the reason companies need to be constantly tracking digital trends. The value in the ongoing tracking of digital trends is to be preemptive, identifying opportunities and iteratively improvements to your business model, not waiting until new competitors have gained enough traction. This is why it has become increasingly common for CEOs and the entire C-suite of global corporations to demand that digital trends be an increasingly heavily weighted factor when updating their business strategy.

Reasons to Monitor Digital Trends

Examining trends in digital is simply a very important *piece* of the larger process of digital transformation. Why is it so important to look at digital trends? When observed consistently, these trends will reveal insights that are extremely applicable to the future of your company and your business model(s). If executed correctly, a good business process around digital trend analysis can even provide "predictive" analytical results for your organization. Specifically, examining digital trends will help you to:

Identify New Business Models

Digital trends do not just expose technologies and consumer behavior, they also reveal new ways of doing business and generating revenue. They can even reveal new economies that you didn't know existed. Tracking digital trends for business model exploration and validation should help you challenge and question how you do business today, and whether or not it is sustainable. For example, the trend of autonomous driving has the potential to completely change the business model of auto insurance. What are auto insurance giants today planning to do about this?

Ward off Disruption

Some digital trends end up being "digital fads" and then go away. Other digital trends end up entirely changing the way people behave and interact with each other—for a long time to come. It's safe to say, for instance, that Facebook and social media is not a fad, but a constantly evolving trend that has changed and will continue to change the way people behave and interact. How many companies has this impacted? How many new businesses has it inspired that have the potential to disrupt it, or play off of it? A close examination of digital trends in social media (or any other area) will give companies a head start on preventing themselves from allowing these changes to disrupt their business.

Better Understand Constituent Behavior

No matter what business you're in, it's very likely your organization interacts with people each day. These people may be consumers or employees, partners or vendors, or contractors or associates. These "constituents" of your business are all using digital differently today than they did 5 years ago and, they'll use digital differently 5 years from now. Understanding their behavior and the changes over time is paramount to being able to serve them. Serving constituents well results in better efficiency, reduced costs, happier employees, partners, and customers.

Predict the Future

The golden unicorn of big data and analytics is to be "predictive." While there is no easy path to being able to make accurate predictions about the future using analytics and trends tracking tools and methods, having a real line of sight to what is coming down the road is certainly possible. Perhaps most famously, predictive analytics has been used in actuarial science for a long time, and continues to get more sophisticated every few years. The next time you are on the phone with your auto insurance company, ask them how they calculated your rate—see if you can get a straight answer. Hint: your driving record nowadays is one of a myriad of factors they use to predict how many times you will get be in an accident in the future.

Applying predictive analytics to digital trends would and could make a powerful combination and while this is not being done effectively today, many smart people and many dollars are being dedicated to the challenge.

Maximize Your Digital Maturity

Back in Figure 4.1, we explored the digital maturity model we use to help large organizations measure where they sit in terms of their sophistication and competitiveness in digital. All companies, in due time, should strive to move up the scale, and maintain themselves once they have reached a high level of digital maturity. Trends analysis is critical to both the acceleration of digital maturity and maintaining a top spot in your industry once you achieve success. Achieving digital maturity is a moving target. You may be competitive now, but you will fall behind over time if you do not work hard to stay there. Trends will help to provide a constant context for where your organization sits on the maturity scale.

Practical Steps to Put Digital Trends to Use

If you want to impact change and results in your organization, digital trends can be a very powerful tool that can accelerate the results

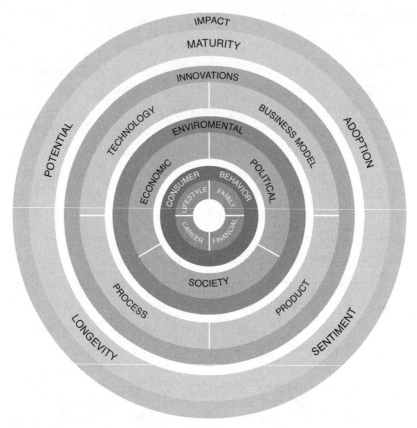

Figure 4.1 Digital trend driver

you want to achieve. However, trends are also a dynamic, complex tool that requires discipline and rigor to use properly. Executives ask us, "how can we realistically keep track of what is happening in digital in any meaningful way?" or "even if we have a method of tracking digital trends, how could we apply that to our situation in a practical, meaningful way?" The answer is with discipline, process and rigor . . . and great contextual visuals. To even consider routinely putting a digital trends dashboard system in place, you have to first know where your company stands today in terms of digital capabilities and performance. Simply put, you need to benchmark yourself—more on this in Chapter 5, but know that you cannot leverage digital trends if you do not know where you stand on the Digital Maturity Scale.

Understanding Trend Drivers

Consumer Behaviors Driving Trends

Consider sites that monitor and analyze consumer behavior. For example, Media Audit's syndicated service measures hundreds of local markets in terms of audiences demographic profiles and media consumption behavior. Another example here is SM2 that monitors online conversations around companies' brands.

Lifestyle Factors

Lifestyle trend sites help people make the shift to a healthier lifestyle. This has opened up multiple opportunities, for example, for Nike to build its Nike Fuel community, for Weight Watchers to thrive online, for Blue Apron for people who want to cook at home but don't have time, to shop or learn to prepare meals from scratch.

Career Factors

More people are now open to freelancing for several companies versus working for one company for a long time. This trend has spurred the growth of sites like Upwork that allow companies to find freelancers with all kinds of skills. These sites help companies find the specialists they need and allow the specialists to find work they do best.

Family and Friend Factors

People are also becoming more open to leverage digital channels to facilitate their personal life. Examples include meeting people online which has driven an explosion in online dating businesses including Match.com, eHarmony and those targeting niche segments such as people meeting later in life at OurTime.com. Many continue to use sites like MeetUp.com to find like-minded peers for socializing, sharing hobbies, and sports activities and interests. And those interested in mapping their family roots are turning to Ancestry.com.

Financial Factors

The global financial crisis has reduced trust in traditional investment management services which has allowed the automated investing services such as Wealthfront, Betterment, Personal Capital, SigFig, and Mint.com.

Environmental Drivers Influencing Trends

Some form of environmental issue touches every industry and consumer either directly or remotely. That's why more businesses are looking for ways to put environmental sustainability at the heart of their existing business models. As businesses start to understand the cost savings that can be realized through minimizing resource use, they're beginning to turn to innovation for sustainability. For instance recyclebank.com offers inspiration and points for people who recycle their paper, plastics, and metal waste.

Economic Factors

The share economy emerged after the 2009 global financial crisis initiated a groundswell of people letting go of the need to own in exchange for stretching their dollars further. A billion dollar industry emerged with the rise in sharing sites for things such as renting rooms or homes using sites like airbnb.com, or tools and household items from sites like neighborgoods.net. The change created by the sharing economy is expected to increase over time as people have successful encounters with Airbnb, Zipcar, Lending Club and other popular sharing economy sites.

Political Factors

"The Revolution will not be televised," while originating as the title of a song/poem from the 1970's, is a revived phrase that encapsulates the type of influence that digital and social media has had on geopolitical events such as the "Arab Spring." The 24/7 availability of news and information sites and desire for less corporate sources of reporting are driving the growth in independent news outlets such as the HuffingtonPost.com, TheDrudgeReport.com, and Salon.com.[1]

Societal Factors

Trends in social sites range according to age, with younger demographics opting for sites like Snapchat.com and Instagram.com. Meanwhile older demographics are becoming more and more active on Facebook. Young professionals still spend the majority of their time on LinkedIn pursuing career opportunities.

Innovations Enabling Trends

Digital technology isn't the only enabling factor of digital transformation. In many cases innovations in business models, product development, and process improvement can be the catalyst.

Technology Innovations

Cloud technology has enabled many traditional models around music (changing from owning it to renting it through streaming rather than downloading it), photos (from storing them in photobooks to sharing them in cloud), and so on.

Business Innovations

Warby Parker is an example of a new business model that cuts out the middleman when it comes to selling eyeglasses. Their business model was innovative in that they eliminated the middleman and went direct to the customer. Their new model allows users to try on glasses in the comfort of their home rather than in a sterile, overpriced brick, and mortar store. The cost is significantly lower and shipping, including returns, is free.

---

[1]http://www.ebizmba.com/articles/political-websites

Product Innovations

As an example of how product innovation could drive a new digital business model, consider Casper.com. Their nationwide fast and free shipping model of shipping mattresses using normal delivery services like FedEx or UPS would not have been possible without their product innovation that allowed their mattresses to be shrunk down into a small box.

Process Innovations

"Next-shoring," the tactic of companies shifting their manufacturing strategies from outsourcing overseas to developing products closer to where they will be sold, allows manufacturers to increase the speed at which their products are replenished on store shelves. Immediacy is the primary factor of digital transformation and next-shoring allows that to happen. Of course the faster inventory can be moved to the consumer, the sooner the costs to warehouse, ship and dock goods can be freed up. This innovative practice is creating a new trend that is emerging to deal with the rise of a more technical labor force needed to manage supply chain operations. Because of rising wages in Asia, higher shipping costs and the need to accelerate time to market to meet retailer and consumer demands and next-shoring appears to be a strong new process trend.

Trend Potential

Wearables is talked about constantly, however to date there is a relatively small impact. But one shouldn't consider the wearables trend beginning and ending with FitBit, Nike Fuel bands, or Apple watches. This trend has significant potential as the concept of wearable expands beyond an additional device to wear or carry and changes to a concept embedded into clothing, accessories and other items you already wear or carry for other reasons.

Just as Kindle was able to jump into the ereader market and dominate it after most publishing giants had written it off, with the right wearable the same thing could happen. It's a trend to pay attention to whether it appears to have relevance to your industry or not. If you're in the hotel business, you're going to be paying attention to Airbnb, but what if you're in the business of supplying hotels with certain supplies? What if you're in the bed manufacturing, or bedding industry, or travel-sized soap and shampoo industry? A disruptor like Airbnb could disrupt your industry.

Trend Magnitude Potential

In 2007 Microsoft's then-CEO, Steve Ballmer, laughed at the iPhone, saying "business users would never go for it, because it doesn't have a keyboard," and, at $500, it "was the most expensive toy in the world."[2] He went on to say, "We're selling millions and millions and millions of phones a year. Apple is selling zero phones a year." Whoops! The iPhone went on to become the greatest disruptor of any device since the computer itself, not only disrupting Research In Motion's (RIM) wildly popular Blackberry phone, but the world of smartphones as well. Most significantly, it changed the entire face of mobile computing and changed the way we interact with each other on a daily basis. Apple had already proven it could capture a huge share of the market with the iPod.

Trend Longevity Potential

Before they pulled out of the wearables market, one of the questions Nike, and other wearables manufacturers asked was, "If you were halfway to work and realized you'd forgotten your fitness tracker, would you turn around and go back for it?" Market research discovered no, most people would not turn around. They'd turn around for their smartphones, but not their fitness trackers. In fact, after 6 months one-third of those who appeared passionate about their devices, would stop wearing their trackers at all.[3] What Nike and other companies have realized is fitness tracker wearables have a very

---

[2] https://www.youtube.com/watch?v=eywi0h_Y5_U&feature=player_embedded

[3] http://endeavourpartners.net/white-papers/

limited appeal—except maybe at New Years when people are making fitness resolutions. There are several reasons for the abandonment:

Fitness trackers are designed to appeal to fitness fanatics, athletes, or would-be athletes. Yet, less than half of Americans exercise. The abandonment rate, Endeavor Partners, a consultancy, noted in a white paper on the topic, "was alarming."[4]

The initial novelty of a tracker is appealing, but it's a trend that doesn't last. That's probably part of the reason that Nike and other manufacturers pulled out of the market and discontinued making fitness trackers. Not only was the market becoming saturated, but the apparent interest from consumers was on what more powerful software could do, not on the wearable itself. What will be interesting to see is who the wearables market disruptor will be.

While wearables is touted as a trend, the hype may be exceeding the technology, at least for now. Smartphones and apps have more appeal, more power, more accuracy, and more capability than most wearables. Until fitness wearables have a higher purpose and a more health-driven technology, like tracking heart rate, blood pressure, blood sugar levels, and so on, long-term appeal of wearables may be limited to the medical industry where wearables like Empatica, a watch that measures the onset of epileptic seizures, are beginning to get investor's attention.[5]

Unlike Nike's Fuelband, which earned the distinction of being the least accurate fitness tracker on the market, medical wearables must be at least 99.999 percent accurate, if not 100 percent accurate. Their data collection must be secure, and quality controls must be so much higher than for a device like a sports watch or pedometer.

Look for fashion conscious wearables, like Cuff.lo, Ringly.com, HelloMemi.com, or others that combine jewelry, headbands, rings, bracelets, and key chains with high-tech and mobile devices to disrupt fitness only trackers.

---

[4] http://endeavourpartners.net/white-papers/

[5] https://www.empatica.com/

Trend Maturity

Where is your company in the technology life cycle? You need to put this in the context in the development of your business. You may have people running up to you shouting, "The internet of things! We've got to get there!" But you might currently be a traditional business just in the beginning of the product lifecycle. Therefore, the IoT currently doesn't have an impact on your business. Or you may be a younger company with limited resources so you can only focus on one area until you grow large enough to drive your business using additional technologies and digital channels. Figure 4.2 illustrates the typical cycle technology runs through and how quickly it is adapted by businesses and put to practical use.

Trend Adoption Stage

System entropy can do a decent job of statistically explain how the typical enterprise is willing to adopt new technology. In Figure 4.3 you can see that only a small percentage of companies are considered to be "innovators" or "early adopters"—meaning they are not many

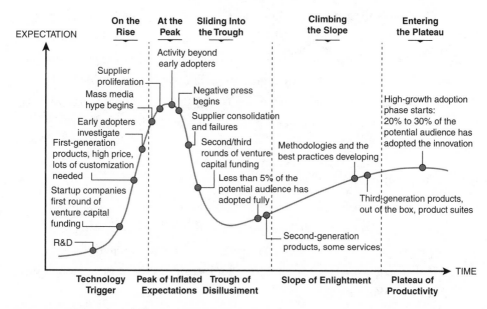

Figure 4.2 Gartner's emerging technology hype cycle

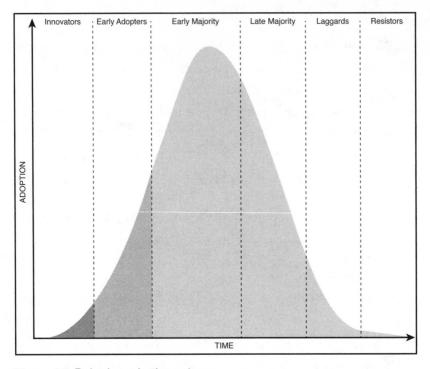

Figure 4.3 Technology adoption cycle

companies willing to stick their next hour and try new technology before it has been proven. The average business falls in the middle to late side of the adoption cycle—we would not advise any company to rush into adoption of any technology. The key to success is to do what is right for *your business* which is why monitoring digital trends and analyzing them, combined with additional disciplines described in this book will drive the best results.

Trend Sentiment

There's a what, where, when, and how to monitor the sentiment of a trend through media (social and traditional). Sentiment is how a group of people respond to a trend. Are people completely excited about it and sharing it on Facebook? Twitter? LinkedIn? Just because someone is saying, "Wearables are changing my life," does not mean you should invest in reaching your customers on their Apple watch. Just because a competitor says, "We couldn't do business without Twitter, or LinkedIn" doesn't mean your company is best served on those social media platforms. You might do better starting your own forum or site where your customers, the ones who are most interested in your product and services, can find like-minded peers. Remember that the right social media can amplify your message, but it can't create it. Sentiment is going to come from the response and reaction of your customers to your message, product and service, and the ease with which they can get what they want.

There are all kinds of listening tools and digital media measurement tools where you can get a pulse or a sentiment analysis of how people are not only thinking about a particular trend, but how fast it's moving. Maybe the magnitude of the trend is coming fast and furious, but the magnitude of what the impact will be is minor. Be aware that measuring sentiment digitally isn't the only, or the best way, to measure a trend.

Monitor Digital Trends

Trend analysis is breaking down a complex whole into smaller parts so you can understand it. It's understanding how and why things changed, or will change, or might change over time.

By breaking down a trend into its various parts, you can see (1) how or if it is relevant to your business, business model, or industry, (2) what parts of the trend can or can't be used with your business model or industry, and (3) where the opportunities lie for your company, your business model or industry, and most importantly trend analysis helps predict where a trend may be headed so your company can be there to greet it when it arrives.

Identify What Matters to Your Company

The first place to start centers around knowing your own industry and the partners, vendors, and other industries you rely upon every day to do business. Who are your vendors? What companies do you partner with to deliver a total solution to your end customer? How does your product end up in the hands of a customer—what does the supply chain look like? Next, as the old business adage goes, know your customers. In the case of analyzing digital trends, knowing your customers means understanding the touchpoints they have with your company and product every step of the way. What is their journey like? How do they find you? Where do they find you? How do they first connect with you? What motivates them to buy from you? How can or do they give you feedback?

Identify Your Customer or Constituent Personas

Collectively you should think about all the individuals and groups that interact with your company as its constituents. All your constituents (whether customer, partner, or vendor) have several things in common as it applies to digital. They all want to interact with your company—and while doing so, have an easy, pleasant experience that enables them to get at what they want quickly.

Identify the Digital Touchpoints Your Customers Most Connect with You Through

Where are your customers experiencing pain or problems in connecting with you? Is it easy to connect, or must they jump through hoops? How many clicks away are you? Why? What technology, social media or purchasing options are they using to buy from you? Those are just some of the trends you need to pay attention to. Look to your analytics and trend analysis for more data to track.

Identify Trend-Related Research and Data Sources

Pay attention to the right data. It's advice that sounds simple, but with a proliferation of the "so-called experts" on the web, it's not. Learn to turn to solid research and data source sites like Forrester, and Gartner, the Pew Center for Research and well-established industry leaders such as eMarketer. We try to stick with a single daily data point and point of view on a digital trend in our blog.

Define a Trend Scoring Model

Create some sort of scoring model that will enable you to quickly find those product initiatives with the most merit. Group your scoring criteria into a few buckets. For example, you might choose buckets such as market size or margin.

Set a Recurring Trend Analyzation Process

It's important to monitor trends and to do so routinely and consistently. Make sure your evaluation and trend monitoring processes focus on your customers' actual expectations, not what you think is important to your customers.

Quantify Trend Opportunities to Prioritize Where to Focus

There isn't necessarily one spot where you *should* jump in. Quantifying opportunity is about understanding where your product is in the Trend Lifecycle. What you may be reading, seeing, and hearing in the press might be caused by the press or the early adopters. You need to calm down and see what the size of the market truly is, how will it realistically get adopted by your business, and when will you really have heavy customer demand.

Action Steps

- Assign someone accountable for trends watching and ensure that person has a direct line to report to leadership.
- Identify the trend drivers that may impact the future of the products and/or services you sell.
- Identify two to three reputable sources of trends information.
- Take time monthly if not weekly to produce/review a trends report.

5

Benchmarking Your Digital Capabilities and Maturity

Before you embark upon a digital transformation, it's critical to know where you currently stand on the digital spectrum, including measuring your strengths and weaknesses. The purpose of this chapter is to help you deconstruct digital and then how to measure your capabilities.

The Layers of Digital Capabilities

Digital is multidimensional and constantly expanding, which can make it hard to measure or self assess. Some companies are confused where the term digital begins and ends. Some consider digital just a technology concept. Some consider it just a marketing concept. Some make the mistake of looking exclusively at certain areas of digital (e.g., social media) to provide an entire representation how well they are performing.

To get a true understanding of how well you are doing and where you need to improve, you need to deconstruct digital into its multiple layers and analyze the various categories. By looking at each layer of digital individually (Figure 5.1), then in conjunction with adjoining and deeper layers, it's easier to understand just how digital can evolve and mature.

We live in a layered world. We get up in the morning and put on underwear, shirts, blouses, ties, jackets, socks, shoes, coats, and

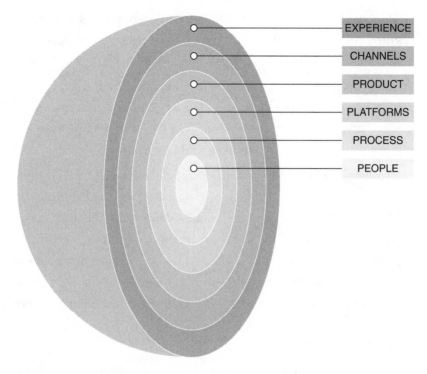

Figure 5.1 Layers of digital

so on according to our job, or what we expect to be doing that day. Each article of clothing serves its own purpose, yet also serves another purpose in conjunction with the adjoining layers. Put your underwear on outside your pants and you not only defeat its purpose, you look strange as well. Socks worn outside your shoes, or a blouse over a jacket defeat the purpose of each item as well as its relationship with the adjoining item.

By deconstructing digital into its layers, functions, and category (outerwear, innerwear, comfort, protection, etc.), it's easy to begin to understand how to interact with the aspects of digital you need for various projects, processes, or strategies.

Also, it's important to understand what you should be comparing yourself to. The question you should be asking yourself isn't, "How do I compare to my competitors?"

It should be more along the lines of, "Where am I on the digital maturity scale? Where do I want to be? How does what my company is doing now compare with what we need to be doing to transform?"

Most importantly, you should be evaluating how what you are doing compares to best practices, setting a benchmark in various areas so you'll have a baseline to work from. You'll be able to objectively see where you actually need to improve and by how much.

To help digest all the dimensions of digital, we've broken them down into seven layers and given primary examples in each layer of what you should be looking at and what best practices you may be comparing your company with. Not every industry uses the same key performance indicator (KPI) or standards. We've used the most broadly used digital capabilities to illustrate the exercise of benchmarking. These aren't intended to be comprehensive layers in all things digital.

Digital Channels

Digital transformation begins with a clear understanding of the channels a company uses to connect with their customers. Different digital channels, whether social media, email, or search, are generally the touchpoints through which brands are most likely to connecting with their customers and where their customers may be connecting with each other (Figure 5.2). Different industries and audiences prefer one channel over another. It's important to not only know that, but to understand why that's so.

Not all channels are relevant to all businesses. Many businesses will vary the mix of focus and investment in these channels depending on what the performance is, what their customer preferences are, and what is the most cost effective. Examples of digital channels and what to benchmark for include the following:

Example: Organic Search Engine Results

Ranking high for your target keyword phrases in organic search results, the listings on search engine results pages that appear because

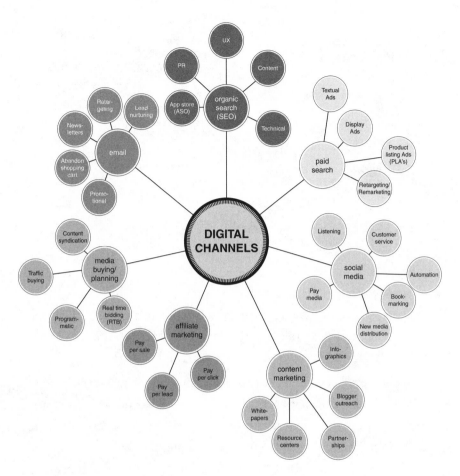

Figure 5.2 Digital channels

of their relevance to your search terms, is the golden unicorn of digital marketing. It is typically very important for companies to do well in organic search. The percentage of most websites traffic that comes from this channel makes it clear why as the Figure 5.3 illustrates.

We tend to prefer websites that perform well organically over those that rely on buying paid search ads as organic search results are designed to be the most direct answer to the user's query, versus paid search which are just another form of advertising. Whenever Google releases an update to their search ranking algorithm, digital businesses will often panic to react to whatever changes were made

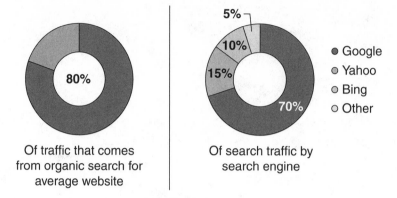

Figure 5.3 Importance of organic search

that impact their ranking and hence their sales assuming a significant amount of their traffic comes from search (which is the case for most companies). As an example, as of the time of this writing, the most recent change Google released was increasing the importance of your website being "responsive" on your search rank.

There are too many factors that contribute to your search rank to name them all in the context of this book. However, there are core strategies that many companies use today to achieve great success in search, such as publishing relevant content containing the appropriate mix of keyword phrases you wish to be found for in search results; generating links from other high authority domain websites focused on your target keyword phrases to your website (sometimes referred to as link building or backlinking); and ensuring your site has the appropriate site structure and content elements so that a text-based search engine could "read" the website, including the appropriate mix of their target keyword phrases throughout their site, images labeled, videos transcribed, and so forth.

In addition, there are many tools out there that can help you measure your performance in this area, including Position.ly and Moz.com.

Example: Social Media

Social media has become a major force in the world of digital but in the context of this book, we're not talking about sharing pictures of what you had for lunch or your vacation. Companies have been using the largest social media networks (Facebook, LinkedIn, Twitter, etc.) to engage with customers, address customer service issues, communicate brand awareness and thought leadership and manage public relations issues, and more. Yet some executives may still scoff off social media as a time waster for millennials; what is lesser known is how much of a factor social media activity and following is in increasing their organic search rankings. According to Search Metric's 2014 report[1] on factors impacting search ranking, social media factors (shares, likes, comments, posts, etc.) account for six of the top ten ranking factors. That's a major although indirect reason for companies to ensure they are doing what they should be in social media. Most companies focus their efforts on two social networks whose purpose and community context best match their brand.

For example, women's clothing retailers may focus on Instagram and Pinterest given the visual nature of their business. Alternatively an enterprise software company may focus more on LinkedIn and Twitter as community there is professional and media and more in the professional mindset. Services like IF This Then That (IFTTT.com) and Onlywire.com can help in automating the distribution of social content to other popular social networks. Similar to search, there are dozens of sources of best practices to use when benchmarking your social media channels.

Other digital channels to benchmark dependent on your industry or business include email, video, affiliate networks, syndicated content, online ad networks, and more.

Digital Ecosystem

Your digital ecosystem is your structured presence or "real estate" in digital, including websites, social media profiles and apps on smartphones, tablets, wearables, Smart TVs, car displays, and other emerging technology touchpoints. Figure 5.4 provides an abstract of how

---

[1] Search Metrics Ranking-Factors 2014 http://www.searchmetrics.com/knowledge-base/ranking-factors/

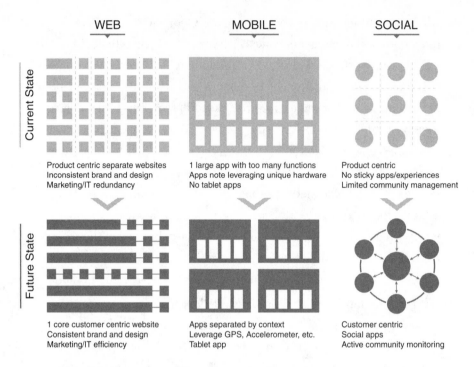

Figure 5.4 Digital ecosystem

many companies structure their web, mobile, and social ecosystems today and where they want to get to in future state.

Examples of categories that companies would benchmark with regards to their ecosystem include:

Example: Mobile App Ecosystem

Some of the most common initial questions people tend to ask when starting to create a mobile strategy are:

- Should we build mobile apps or responsive websites?
- What goes in a mobile app versus the responsive website?
- Should we have more than one mobile app?
- How do we divide features between multiple apps?
- Which mobile operating systems should we support?

There are varying views as to what is best practice in the questions mentioned previously. As far as having more than one app and how to divide features, some brands choose to follow the multiple, single-purpose mobile app ecosystem model where you have an app for each use case. Google is the most prominent demonstration of this strategy. If you look at their apps, there is one app for each of their products, including Gmail, Google Calendar, Google Maps, Google News, Google Docs, Google Wallet, Google Analytics, Google Hangout, and so on. This makes sense as these apps support very different user scenarios. Another approach to structuring a mobile ecosystem is the single multipurpose app.

Starbucks, on the other hand, is an example where one company (in this case quite large) has only one app with all the really critical features in it, including rewards, payment, location finder, news, and more. A third example is the hybrid model, used by the likes of American Express, where there is a combination of a multipurpose app for all the core use cases and one or more single-purpose app for unique use cases that may or may not be replicated in the core application. Some companies using this approach appear to be heading the direction of unbundling their multipurpose app into multiple single-purpose apps.

An example of a poorly implemented mobile ecosystem happened when Hertz launched an app called Hertz 24/7 for their hourly rental cars, separate from their standard daily rental cars in their core app. These seemingly identical apps, however, have failed to educate consumers about their separate functionality. Users are coming to the app for one thing only—to rent a car. Time of car rental is not enough of a determinant to make users switch between applications when the mission of Hertz is singular (to rent cars). Instead, Hertz would be better suited having an option for hourly car rentals within the one umbrella app, similar to how Zipcar users only get charges a flat day rate once they reserve over a certain number of hours in one day. On the other hand, airlines like Delta have done a good job integrating all their use cases into one multipurpose app, largely in part because they understand the

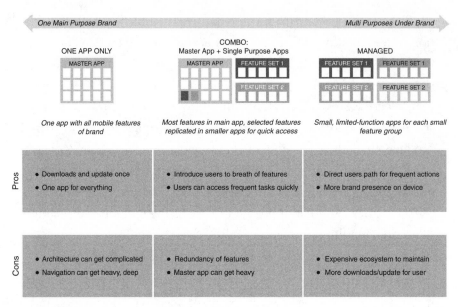

Figure 5.5 Mobile app ecosystem framework

customer journey. Booking a flight, checking flight time, and locating your boarding pass are combined in one efficient app. Figure 5.5 has visuals of the possible mobile app frameworks your company can create.

Example: Websites Ecosystem

It is easy to get caught up in the mobile app frenzy. However, given the time and investment that one must put into app development, many companies are wise to simply invest more in their responsive website apart from a core app. From an ecosystem perspective, companies with multiple business units, product lines, countries, languages, and more struggle with having multiple websites and even more campaign sites, minisites, and landing pages. This is typically a legacy issue stemming from less flexible technology that prevented marketers from quickly launching new content or capabilities to a core website. Rather than wait and miss an opportunity, they simply created a new website.

Obviously from a customer perspective, this can be confusing. From a search perspective, they are missing domain authority by having separate websites. From an operations standpoint, there is tremendous redundancy in platforms and typically disconnected experiences. This can result in your best customers, those who use more than one product, being treated the worst by being forced to go to multiple websites. Many companies looking to achieve best practices are working on integrating their websites under one domain and putting in a navigation system that will allow for different user groups to find what they are looking for easily.

Example: Social Media Profiles

From an ecosystem perspective, it's recommended that you secure your brand on all social profiles. One challenge companies experience with social profiles is that because it's so easy to set up a profile, any employee or customer can do it. For example, a company named ABC Corporation may setup its core social media profiles under its main name. But there isn't much to stop "rogue" employees in a business unit from setting up other profiles specific to their business unit. And depending on the social network, there is little to stop customers or people not affiliated with the company from setting up profiles or groups as well. The result is well-known brands may have many redundant social profiles, which further confuses customers that may be searching for them on a particular social network.

As an example, search on Twitter for a common Fortune 100 company name and see how many profiles come back. There is usually at least one that is verified. There may also be multiple variations. From a customer perspective, it may not be very clear which one you should be looking for. A similar search in Facebook, LinkedIn, and other prominent social networks will give similar results. This doesn't mean you should remove all the multiple accounts. However, if there is a justification for having multiple profiles, it needs to be made very clear on each profile what its purpose is and how to find the correct profile they are looking for if the one they are currently on isn't it.

Digital Experience

By *experience* we are referring to the customer experience. This encompasses the collective of the interactions between your customers and your company. This is most often from online experiences, but the customer experience can include offline experiences as well. Companies that create experiences that are unique from those of their competitors, while also responding effectively and timely to their customers' wants and needs, are seen as having created successful customer experiences.

Example: Omnichannel Experience

It's not enough to provide a smooth, effective user experience anymore. Companies with multiple customer channels are being pressured to provide an integrated experience as well. Multichannel services are requiring complex digital changes across both the online customer experience and the internal operational processes. For instance, most major retailers, including Barnes & Noble, Target, Staples, Wal-Mart, and even Lowes, now offer home shopping with the option to receive products by mail or via pickup in your local store. Retailers report customers become upset when customer service representatives in a store can't access their online order history. Others are peeved when a store can't tell them the number on their customer loyalty cards, or reorder a new card in order to keep their discounts and coupons. The customer rightfully views every touchpoint as integrated with every other touchpoint in a cohesive organization. You must do the same.

A successful retail omnienvironment is one that will seamlessly meld "the advantages of in-store (brick and mortar) shopping with the information-rich experience of online shopping." An integrated experience will enhance the company brand and experience the company wants for its customers, no matter what channel they access it through. Making shopping seamless for your customers pays off. According to an RIS News white report on "Omnichannel Readiness," retailers estimated a 6.5 percent loss of revenue due to the lack of successfully integrating a true omnichannel strategy, while those who do create a true omnichannel experience stand to gain millions.[2]

According to Forrester, ecommerce makes about $200 billion in revenue in the United States and is forecasted to reach $327 billion by 2016.[3] ABI research has estimated that by 2015, shoppers worldwide will spend about $119 billion on goods purchased on a mobile phone.[4] In the same RIS News report, only 19.2 percent of retailers have successfully adopted an omnichannel solution, 30.8 percent of retailers are changing strategies and catching up. But 50 percent of retailers are behind, and have no plans to change.

Crate & Barrel (C&B) is well known for their omnichannel experience. They know that customers conduct research online, pin items from Pinterest, discuss items on Facebook, and check in on their mobile devices before shopping. So the C&B app saves their shopping cart so they can access their information across multiple devices and browsers. No matter where a C&B customer is in their shopping or checkout process, they don't have to reenter their billing, buying, or shopping information.

Another popular feature C&B offers is a seamless experience for customers who want to use their wedding and gift registry, allowing shoppers to create and manage their registries from their mobile phone.

Then there are Starbucks customers who have the option of checking and reloading their Starbucks card through their phone, the Starbucks website, or while they're at the store. Customers can

---

[2] Skorupa, J. RIS, News Custom Research. (2013). *Omnichannel readiness*

[3] Indvik, L. (2012, February 27). U.S. online retail sales to reach $327 billion by 2016. *Mashable*

[4] ABI, New York Business Wire. (2010) Shopping by MobileWill Grow to $119 Billion.   http://www.businesswire.com/news/home/20100216006723/en/Shopping -Mobile-Grow-119-Billion-2015-ABI#.Vbx5T0UnYqg

pay for product with either their rewards card or their phone or mobile device. Balances are automatically updated across all channels as well.

Brides shopping for wedding dresses can use the Alfred Angelo "magic mirror" app by PicknTell. The app works with mobile devices which link to a special mirror, which videotapes future brides trying on wedding dresses. The app then forwards the video and photos to selected friends and family in real time, allowing them to share in the wedding dress selection process.[5]

Example: Responsive Website Design

As the first Internet-enabled devices hit the market and before the concept of app stores, digitally savvy companies like Amazon. com all started creating websites separate from their core website. These websites were specially designed to fit smaller screen sizes, as well as the input controls of a mobile device. These sites are typically referred to a company's mobile website or "m-dot" site. This required companies to maintain at least two redundant websites—redundant content, redundant features, redundant experiences. As mobile browsers, website design, and development have evolved, the concept of responsive design has emerged.

Responsive website design allows companies to create one website with one source of content. It's now possible to leverage front-end technology like CSS (Cascading Style Sheets) to change not only the content layout, but the content and features being displayed. Because technology "knows what device and screen size is being used by the user, whether it's a web browser on a desktop computer, a web browser on a tablet, or a web browser on a smartphone, the website responds with the appropriate size screen."

Additional best practices may include adaptive design which presents an entirely different design, content or feature depending

---

[5] http://www.pickntell.com/web/retailer/

on what device is being used. For example, a feature or content that leverages the specific hardware capabilities of a smartphone such as an accelerometer, a device that measures acceleration, may only show up on the website when the user is on a smartphone. However, it won't show up on when viewed through a web browser on a desktop.

Example: Website and Application Navigation System

One of the current mainstream trends in navigation design is the hamburger menu, a stack of three bars typically located in the top right, or sometimes top left of a website. Once clicked, these bars open up a menu. This approach is considered a best practice as it can be used consistently on a responsive website whether it's the smartphone version or the desktop website version. Effective navigation design is about setting up a website to guide readers through it as simply as possible so that they know what content is available, and where to find what they are looking for. This means including things like breadcrumbs, navigation elements, filters, laddering, layered navigation, primary menu, sitemaps, sorting, and personalization.

Like navigation design, site organization arranges content on a website in such a way as to be as user friendly as possible so users can find the information they need. It includes content-to-commerce linking, footer content, site-wide content organization, and on-page content organization.

Digital Features

Example: Customization

Customization allows users to choose how they interact with a website, including setting communication preferences and content preferences. The important focus here should be tools that enable your customers to add their own unique, personalization to their customer experience when using your site.

Example: Account Management

Set up website accounts so users get the most information as simply as possible. Accounts can include alerts and notifications, dashboard, loyalty programs, account settings, order management, password reset, username lookup, payment and shipping preferences, user account registration, and shopping cart.

Example: Customer Service

Everyone knows what good customer service looks like in the brick and mortar world but how does that translate to the online world and what might be your emphasis here? According to our research, the winner is live chat versus email.[6]

Digital Platforms

Next, what platform or platforms have you created where you are seen so others can connect/see/engage with you? How strong is your digital platform? Your goal is to create a powerful platform where other *businesses* can easily connect their *business* with yours, build products and services on top of it, and co-create value. Examples of typical platforms that many digital businesses will benchmark include the following.

Example: Analytics

Digital is more measurable than most channels. The analytics solutions out there give any marketer or digital business owner the ability to really drive business decisions based on facts and not assumptions. Historically larger organizations have used the likes of Omniture and WebTrends which offer very robust capabilities; however, we're finding more and more that organizations are relying on Google Analytics. Whatever analytics solution you choose, what's important is to have

---

[6] http://www.jdpower.com/press-releases/2013-us-wireless-customer-care-full-service-performance-study-volume-2-and-2013-us

an analytics platform implemented and your team actively using it to analyze digital business performance, including the success of campaigns, transformation initiatives, and site enhancements.

More sophisticated analytics teams are also stacking additional platforms like Kissmetrics, Mixpanel, Segment.io, and Flurry Analytics to get a deeper understanding into A/B testing, segmentation, customer journeys, and conversion. With all these different analytical tools, you may also want to incorporate a dashboard tool to provide summary visual dashboards for your executive team and any key stakeholders that don't have time to sift through the details. Examples of current dashboarding tools include Domo, Tableau, and Qlikview.

Analytics isn't just for marketers and business managers. Data savvy user experience experts are incorporating analytics tools like CrazyEgg to better visualize their customers' behavior on their website pages using features such as heat-maps. Leveraging these tools and iterating revisions based on the results helps companies more quickly incorporate real customer feedback into their digital experience as opposed to the elongated processes of focus groups and wireframe testing before launch. It's also possible that what people are saying they would do isn't what they will actually do.

Example: Multivariate Testing

Websites and mobile apps are made of combinations of changeable elements. Multivariate testing changes two or more of those elements, creating various versions of the elements which are then tested to determine the best or most optimized version. Many tools exist to help digital businesses do this, including Optimizely, Adobe Target, Unbounce, and GetResponse.

Example: Personalization Engine

Oracle studies show 81 percent of people are willing to spend more time and money with a merchant when their shopping experience is more personalized.[7] With people becoming more and more digitally adept, the need to constantly recreate your customer experience is a necessity. Implementing a personalization engine is a critical platform to optimize your online business. This technology creates a unique experience for each customer on each visit. It tailors the site as the customer shops, customizes communications to the customer, and increases revenue with recommendations. The focus here should be on collaboration/preference targeting, demographic targeting, device-based targeting, location IP/GEO targeting, on-site behavioral targeting, profile-based targeting, retargeting campaign management, rule management tools, rules/expression-based targeting, and segment management tools.

Benchmark Your Capabilities

A company could have all the right platforms and still not use them well. This is where benchmarking comes in. Benchmarking will help set a standard by which you can measure the right elements of your transformation efforts. Digital benchmarks will provide points of reference to tell you where you stand with your own digital transformation in relation to other companies' transformation initiatives, company goals, or industry standards. Benchmarks also offer the baseline by which you can judge your performance, set goals or use to make strategic decisions, or create business models from. Benchmarks tell you how well, or how poorly, you're performing so you can make needed adjustments. Think of a benchmark report as a dashboard on a car—telling you what the status of your vehicle is. How good are your current resources (oil and gas gauges), your temperature (hot/cold), and what kind of mileage are you getting, and what speed are you moving at?

Anchor to a Digital Maturity Scale

Where exactly you'll want to go through depends on where you currently are. There are several stages on the road to full digital

---

[7] http://www.oracle.com/us/corporate/press/1883120

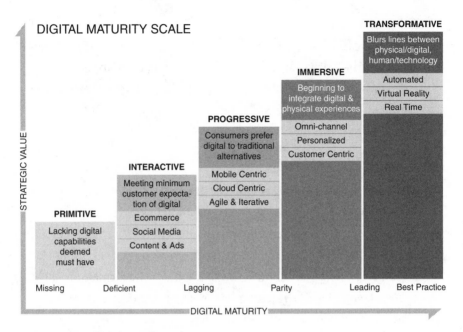

Figure 5.6 Digital maturity scale

maturity, the ideal status of any company wanting to lead in its field (Figure 5.6).

Primitive Digital Maturity

Companies like these are missing very basic digital components like social media presence and mobile websites, making them irrelevant, if not invisible, to most of today's consumers. This stage exemplifies a complete absence of digital maturity.

Reactive Digital Maturity

Meeting the bare minimum of customer expectation regarding digital earns you the status of "interactive" or "reactive." You could have an ecommerce platform, for instance, but it might be one that is difficult to use or unfriendly with mobile. Interactive companies display some digital maturity, but it's still deficient. This is a normal stage for many companies. They aren't aware there's a name for what they're seeing their competitors do digitally. A competitor's digital success is often their wake-up call and what prompts them to react. They either continue to react, playing catch-up, like Blockbuster reacted to Netflix's renting movie DVDs and streaming movies. Or, they stop and commit to a digital transformation.

Progressive Digital Maturity

A progressive company is well on its way to digital maturity, but it's still lagging behind some of the top companies in its space. These companies typically use a mobile-first approach, rely heavily on cloud technologies, and quickly remove any reported bugs or bottlenecks. This stage involves committing to a digital transformation. That includes, developing a strategic plan by accumulating and assessing the data and information you already have about your customers. It means studying the market and then developing the best strategy to achieve your goals for your company. This involves incorporating digital, considering your "mobile-first" approach and implementing changes that will ultimately propel your organization into a true digital transformation. Your products or services may remain the same, but the changes in how they're sold become significant.

Immersive Digital Maturity

At this stage, a company can be said to have reached digital maturity, keeping more at-pace with the digital landscape than almost all of its competitors. Immersive businesses have begun to integrate physical and digital to create omnichannel experiences for their customers and use digital tools to personalize those experiences as much as possible.

Transformative Digital Maturity

Beyond digital maturity, these companies are the leaders and innovators in their field for their mastery of tech. Processes are often fully automated, and the lines between human and technology have been blurred completely. Companies like these might be implementing technology like virtual reality or driverless vehicles to augment their services.

Everyone wants to be transformative in their sector, a company that permanently and completely changes how their business is done. But reaching that kind of mastery takes time, investment, and plenty of risk. Before you can lead the shift in how businesses everywhere work, you have to make sure your own company does what it's supposed to in the most efficient way possible. This stage is the end result of the innovation of your business. At this point, you understand and have implemented technology that allows your organization to interact with your customer base in ways you never could have before the transformation. When done properly, digital transformation enables your organization to stay relevant and competitive year after year.

Benchmark Best Practices, Not Just Competitors

Look beyond how the leading companies in your industry do digital. Don't get trapped into just following your competitors or your industry. Break out. Instead, focus on your own unique experiences and resources that include your channels, features, ecosystem, platform, processes, and people. Think about what you could combine to make up your unique value mix of offerings. Decide what's most important to you.

As a recent Harvard Business article points, the best ideas for your industry won't always come from your industry. In fact, "Bringing in ideas from analogous fields turns out to be a potential source of radical innovation."[8]

If you are looking for radical innovation—and who isn't, then start looking at innovations *outside* rather than inside your marketplace." The authors further share that, counter intuitively, the more distant the sources you tap for help in innovating are from your industry the more

---

[8] https://hbr.org/2014/11/sometimes-the-best-ideas-come-from-outside-your-industry

novel their ideas. It's in the novelty of their ideas that the better ideas are created. Why? According to the authors, successful results come from "people who aren't constrained by the assumed limitations and mental schemas of your own professional world."[9] So when you are looking for new opportunities, consider taking the adage one of our colleagues often shares with her clients, "A billion dollar business was born when chocolate collided with peanut butter." Where can you look outside of your own backyard to find a billion-dollar collision of opportunity?

Another way to gain innovative insight is to look for experts in digital transformation with whom you can share your industry expertise and, in turn, receive their digital expertise. This complement of skills should also go a long way to helping you see things that might not have been self-evident during their own industry reviews. This comes from the concept "you don't know what you don't know." Second, you're the business. Pair your organization with the right digital marketing masters that's where the magic happens.

Focus on Capabilities You Need to Win in

There are hundreds if not thousands of digital capabilities that could be analyzed. However, not all capabilities are relevant to your company. For example, banks would need to excel in different capabilities versus a healthcare company versus a retailer. So look at the elements that matter to your industry.

Repeat the Benchmark Regularly

Your benchmark will change anytime you change any of your digital capabilities or when what is considered a best practices is taken to the next level. If you haven't changed anything over time, your benchmark will inevitably get worse. To keep up with the changing world of digital, you may want to consider regular benchmarks (at minimum annually and perhaps even quarterly).

---

[9] Ibid.

Action Steps

- Identify the digital capabilities that are critical to your business within all the layers of digital.

- Identify best practices for those capabilities.

- Identify your digital competitors and companies you'd like to emulate in digital.

- Compare your capabilities to best practices and competitors and score yourself relative to the digital maturity scale.

- Figure out where you need to be on the digital maturity scale at the capability level.

6

Envisioning Your Digital Strategy

When we say "get your strategy off the page," we're not talking about giving up presentations entirely. In today's digital world though there are many companies that still conduct business in this now more traditional way but there is a more interactive, immersive way to proceed when it comes to digital initiatives.

Getting your strategy off of the PowerPoint page is about not only changing the game as to how you implement your digital strategy within your organization, but how you communicate it.

Once you begin to change the way you communicate your digital rollout with team members and other stakeholders, and, in turn, they adopt new communication tools, you will become more proficient at deploying newer, more effective strategies and tactics. As a result, you will develop a culture that is more agile and digitally transformative.

By implementing your initiatives using digital tools, you will get a better end result faster as you cut out those wordy slides and, instead, create working prototypes that will more effectively grab the attention and buy in from your stakeholders and, in turn, shorten your strategic planning and product development cycle dramatically.

Profile Your Digital Audience
A New Model to Understand Your Audience

A digital transformation means you have to change your focus, angle, or perspective. When you approach your customer through

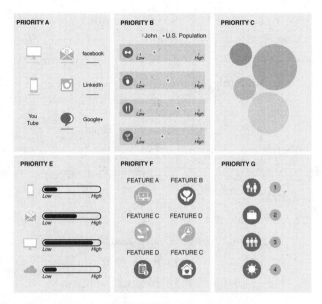

Figure 6.1 Example of a digital audience profile

a digital lens—whether you use your own analytics or those of a competitor—you're changing what you see. You're trying to understand how they would potentially process your digital messages versus your traditional non-digital communications. You see your customers in a new way, and they will eventually do the same with you as your company begins its transformation (Figure 6.1).

Are they using smartphones to access your site? Do they want to? How much time are they spending in various social media channels? Do they prefer LinkedIn, Twitter, or Facebook? Are they active Instagram or Pinterest users? Do they prefer information about your product coming in an email, or would they rather connect with a webinar?

Knowing customer preferences helps you determine the delivery system that will best resonate with them. In the past, you may have used focus groups or surveys to understand how customers found you or purchased from you. Now, by creating a new model for profiling your audience, you can define what touchpoints, channels, and devices they use, as well as accumulate a variety of data about them. Knowing where and how customers find you is important because that's where you'll be communicating with them most. Those channels will also dictate how you communicate—video versus mobile app for instance.

Digital communication by its nature is what we call a "visually tactile" concept—meaning understanding the digital communication results from experiencing it in whatever model a company chooses to use to express itself.

For example, Nike doesn't say, "Tell your friends about us." They give you a wearable or a mobile app that lets you easily send your friends updates, photos, and data about your run. They know it's hard for most people to visualize a 5K run, so they provide an app with a digital map, with your 5K run progress lit up like a neon pathway. The customer can see at a glance that they did indeed bust it running around Central Park and back home, and they can choose to share that with select friends.

So, with all the tools, apps, and devices that make it possible to inspire, amaze, astound, and astonish, why do so many companies continue to communicate their strategy with a text wall of "corporate-speak" and PowerPoint presentations?

When was the last time you were inspired by a PowerPoint presentation to the point you wanted to laugh, cheer, or stand up and run a mile? More importantly, when's the last time you wanted to share a PowerPoint presentation? Yet, if a friend were to message you a challenge to compete with them in a new weight loss contest, how tempted would you be to text back and say "bring it!?"

Your customer is either experiencing a rush of desire to engage with you in some way, or they're looking for someone else who will. Which will it be?

While older communication methods can be adequate for certain outcomes, using tools that create newer forms of digital assets can be transformational for your organization. These tools aren't just novel toys or cool apps. They're how a digitally native population, that includes employees as well as customers, communicate.

When an organization's team members become familiar with these new tools, it will influence the culture of your organization. These tools drive accuracy, which forces a shift in mindset that's more conducive to a digital transformation.

Put a Digital Lens on Your Customer Segments

Look at your customer segments, not just by their age, location, or income. These are all important things that traditional marketing teams should still be doing. You've looked at how many customers own a cell phone, or are using an iPad versus a desktop versus another mobile device. Now expand your digital lens to discover other touch-points along the way that cause people to engage.

Think about *when* they engage. Are you a company they seek out when they're traveling (hotel, gas station, restaurant), or on weekends (DIY, movies, entertainment, clubs, bars). Are you a scheduled stop (dentist, doctor, accountant) or an impulse purchase (e.g., retail, entertainment, fast food).

Align Users' Needs and Business Goals

One of the primary steps in the process of *aligning* your business goals with your customers is to make sure you're designing for who your customers actually are, not who you think they might be.

Anytime you are *defining* strategies, align them with your goals, otherwise you may end up with a situation where users want to access content for free, but the business wants to make money on it. This is what happened with *The New York Times* when it kept jockeying between giving away all their content for free versus charging for everything and then not showing up in SEO searches.

Ultimately *The Times* created a kind of middle ground where they now give away about 10 articles a month. If a user wants more news or articles, he or she can pay for a subscription. This should be your goal—to find the right balance in order to create alignment. *The Times* is an example of a traditional business that is trying to transform itself.

Identifying and aligning the needs of users with your organization's goals begins with creating and analyzing your customers' daily journey map. Where do they find you? Organic or paid search? Word of mouth or advertisement? As a leader and communicator, your employees expect you to see patterns, trends, and business opportunities before they become evident to others.

Customers want and expect you to communicate with them in a way they understand and find seamless and simple. They'll buy in when you make it easy for them to do so. Employees begin to buy in to your vision when you communicate it well enough that they get the vision and want to be part of it. Get people involved in the process, and they begin to take ownership. Deliver your vision and your strategy in an interactive format and it will be an easier sell. People will also be more willing to participate and contribute to the concept and the ideas if you give them access to the process in an agile way, where they can "own" the idea from the beginning.

Let's say you're delivering a strategy to your executive team, Board of Directors, whoever it may be. Instead of showing them a slideshow with bullet points and sketches, try handing them a workable 3D prototype where they can actually experience the future of the device or software. It might be an interactive graphic, a video representation, a 3D mockup from different vantage points, or even a colorful "map" of your proposed process. You don't need a database or a polished prototype in the perfect color with the logo. All you need is a working prototype with strong components that function well enough to give your audience the chance to actually experience the idea or strategy firsthand.

By getting your executive team or board of directors involved with a working prototype in the early stages of digital development, you create a connection and desire in them to see the device finalized. The experience also sparks innovation, ideas, and participation.

After they've played with the device for a while they're more likely to say, "What about adding _____," or "What if we do _____?" They've stopped being passive, sideline observationalists, and started absorbing your vision and are now participating in the process, strategy, and development. And remember, you will be using agile methodology across your development team, so generating prototypes quickly should not be a problem.

Journey Map Your Experience

Journey maps are like the people—no two are alike, yet they consistently work to tell you what you want to know about how your customer finds you, explores your services, and decides to buy from you. It also tells you why they decide to continue to buy from you, and whether or not they will return for other products or purchases. While customer experiences will vary, the patterns and channels they utilize will remain fairly consistent. Begin journey mapping your omnichannel experience through a series of steps:

- Review the goals for product or service.
- Gather your research: Interviews, surveys, logs, analytics, and other tools.
- Generate a list of touchpoints.

Your Journey Map and Your User Base

How digitally savvy is your user base? Perhaps you don't realize your audience is visiting you 30 percent more on mobile devices—smartphones and tablets—than from a desktop computer. If your site is heavy in downloads, you may have already lost your mobile audience, or never had them to begin with. Knowing your users digital usage profile will help you reimagine your communication delivery methods.

Creating a digital lens on top of their usage profile will allow you to see if the newer communication delivery system is more effective or not. If customers are visiting your site more frequently from a mobile device like a tablet, ask yourself why?

For example, take hotels that partner with neighboring restaurants, gyms, spas, and retail stores to offer their hotel guests a discount for shopping those stores. This may be the conduit that enables their traffic spiking with out-of-town shoppers.

IT issues can drive a spike in web traffic, but so can press releases, celebrity endorsements, weather, tragedy, a television show, or a mention in a popular blog can spike your traffic. So how can you ensure that your delivery system is best optimized for those visitors?

Because most digital experiences are multichannel, you want to map out your user's journey. By using journey maps, you'll recreate and understand their current informational experience and identify ways to modify or enhance it into a better one. Start with their current journey. Are there channels that have been bypassed but may now be effective? Could a message be strengthened or supported with an additional component or channel? Multiple touchpoints can reinforce a message for greater buy-in. Journey maps are about visualizing what you are seeing—whether it's the clickable or experience prototypes. Is there a different route by which your viewers will have a more meaningful experience?

Take, for example, a digital initiative Nike reworked when their analytics revealed that their male and female users wanted different things in their apps and their journeys. So they launched Nike Training Club for Women, utilizing workouts, drills, and content targeted at women as a supplement for its Nike Women website.[1] They changed their strategy based on their customer's journey map.

Keep researching your customer base. Pinterest, for example, has 80 percent more female users and draws 400 percent more revenue

---

[1] http://mashable.com/2010/12/06/nike-training-club-iphone/

than Twitter.[2] Monitoring gender behavior isn't about reinforcing gender stereotypes. It's about using data to find out what really makes your audience tick. By using digital tools to continuously assess your users and their needs, you will gain a better perspective on their digital journey.

Identify Key Touchpoints

Touchpoints are the critical elements that connect a customer with your organization. For example, a touchpoint might be your product's packaging, your website, a chat with your representative on a social media channel, or even the experience of walking into your brick and mortar store. What you're looking for in a touchpoint experience is anything that provides a point of contact or opportunity for a customer to discover, shop, buy, and either develop loyalty to your business, or to seek a solution elsewhere.

Understanding or creating a customer persona, such as the needs, goals, thoughts, feelings, opinions, expectations, and pain points of the user is helpful; as is defining the amount of time you expect a customer to spend with you. For example, a customer buying groceries is going to visit a grocery store website more regularly over time than one buying a car.

Create a finite timeline for the customer experience—from a day to a week, month, or a year. Take into account the emotional aspects of the journey—confusion, frustration, joy, pain, regret, buyer's remorse, or celebratory feelings. Finally, note the touchpoints—what is the customer doing, and where this action is taking place? Are they emailing the company? Are they calling customer service with questions or complaints? Are they posting about their experience on social media, visiting the store? How and where are they interacting? Is the experience primarily digital or physical or both?

---

[2] https://www.sprinklr.com/social-scale-blog/targeting-genders-social-data-insights-stereotypes/

Identifying/Defining Use Cases

How do your customers interact with your company to solve a problem they have? It's necessary to create a use case or a written narrative of all the steps your customer must take to make a purchase or get the information they wanted from your company or website. Use cases include a list of actions around:

- Who is using the website?
- What the user wants to do?
- The user's goal.
- The steps the user takes to accomplish a particular task.
- How the website should respond to an action?

Write the steps in a use case in an easy-to-understand narrative. First, identify an actor (customer), the basic flow of the event, and then the specific steps to the event, triggers for the event, and alternative scenarios for the event. Kenworthy outlines the following steps:[3]

1. Identify who is going to be using the website.
2. Pick one of those users.
3. Define what that user wants to do on the site. Each thing the user does on the site becomes a use case.
4. For each use case, decide on the normal course of events when that user is using the site.
5. Describe the basic course in the description for the use case. Describe it in terms of what the user does and what the system does in response that the user should be aware of.
6. When the basic course is described, consider alternate courses of events and add those to "extend" the use case.
7. Look for commonalities among the use cases. Extract these and note them as common course use cases.
8. Repeat the steps two through seven for all other users.

---

[3] http://www.usability.gov/how-to-and-tools/methods/use-cases.html

Once you've defined your Use Cases, you can map the user journey/experience within your communication structure, identifying stopping points, potential dead-ends, or abandonments as well as successful completion of a desired outcome: for example, a sale or a request for more information.

Defining Enterprise Digital Strategy

An enterprise digital strategy is a business strategy that services all business units, not just one. For example, a bank has a credit card division, a mortgage division, a business loans unit, and so on. The mortgage division may have their own digital strategy that works as does the credit card division. Now you have more than one business unit, both of whom are using the same strategy, but the two don't connect, so consumers must go to a number of different locations to get their needs met. As a result they have a consistently poor user experience, even though a digital strategy, of sorts, exists.

On the other hand, let's say you implement an enterprise digital strategy that integrates all the bank's digital units. Now bank users are able to have an integrated account-managed experience with a single sign on for all of their products with one content management system, and so on. This integrated model is critical because, otherwise, companies will continue to lose their customer base when they create redundant capabilities.

Enterprise digital strategy thinks about all the products and all the services an organization offers and works to house them in one location so that they don't build redundant user experiences. Many of these kinds of redundant units are the case for a lot of banks. The business units will push back wanting to protect their turf. While they all know the key to digital maturity is centralizing offerings, too many banks are still late in becoming digitally adept.

Gartner predicts that this lack of digital business competence will cause 25 percent of businesses to lose competitive ranking by 2017.

Furthermore, they say that CIOs and IT professionals who think digital business is synonymous with IT are going to be blindsided.[4]

In other words, if you don't understand what digital strategy is, or how to utilize it, you're not going to succeed in a digital marketplace. A digital strategy requires a thorough understanding not only of products and services, but of digital touchpoints, journey maps, technology, analytics, and company visions and goals. Before you can even begin to define your digital strategy, you have to understand it.

Following are considerations to take into account when defining your strategy:

- Start with your digital vision and objectives and align them with your goals.
- Set up measurements for the impacts of each initiative.
- Develop a concise process for rolling out your plan.

The Importance of Visualizing Strategy

"Show me," is the rallying cry of digital customers in a digital world. They aren't content to just read about or hear what you have to say. In a world where you can link them to a video, a demonstration, a podcast, photo, or interactive chart, why wouldn't you show them? Having a working prototype that allows future users and your stakeholders to experience it is even better. If you're serious about effective strategy, you're serious about creating prototypes to speed the development and strategy along. Customers report they're more likely to spend more time and money when a shopping experience is personalized.[5]

If your strategy is to have people reorder your laundry detergent rather than try a new brand, think about putting a sensor on the bottle that alerts the owner that supplies are low. Or, follow Amazon's lead—with the Amazon Dash—a button you press when you want to order

---

[4] http://www.gartner.com/newsroom/id/2745517

[5] Skorupa, J. RIS, News Custom Research. (2013).*Omnichannel readiness*

more of something, whether it's coffee, dog food, detergent, or vitamin supplements. Being able to have a working prototype helps you develop your strategy because you're more likely to find additional touchpoints where you can reach your customers.

Visual Stories Pack More Details into Easily Digested and Sharable Information

Visuals are King. Digital companies understand this and are on board with the change from text to graphics. This doesn't mean you turn to a designer on day one, have them draw a picture and you're done. It's not about converting everything you say to photos and infographics. Yes, visual is powerful, but only when it's part of a larger strategy and carries a memorable and visceral message.

You still have to figure out the opportunity and the other elements of the strategic rollout, but at the end of the day, the best ways to present your ideas are in a much more visual form.

Leverage Strategic Frameworks

A "framework" is a visual model for strategic themes. The framework you'll need for your transformation should contain just the basic tools you'll have to assemble or acquire to create a great and unique customer experience. "There are no rules" because no two companies are the same. There are best and common practices. Also, every industry is different so every framework is different. Successful digital companies develop their own frameworks to best suit their own digital DNA. The pharmaceutical industry, for instance, will have a different framework than a transportation industry or an apparel manufacturer, or an athletic gear retailer.

Create Rapid Prototypes
How to Bring Your Strategy to Life Quicker

Showing people your strategy is far more effective than telling them what your strategy is. According to the Social Science

Research Network, 65 percent of us are visual learners that we learn best through the use of images. Have you wondered why the use of infographics has exploded in the last several years? There's a reason! Visual elements like photos and videos get far more play in social media. Why? Because they're pictorial. Photos, infographics, charts, diagrams—they're all designed to create that "aha!" moment.

Text-heavy blog posts, white papers, and bulleted PowerPoint slides are harder to grasp, require the viewer to have a context, or create one, to understand the message. They're also time consuming to prepare and read. That's why infographics, charts, photos, and diagrams go viral and blog posts and texts and bullet-pointed PowerPoint slides turn into credenza-ware.

Seeing information in a format that provides concepts, facts, and data in visual soundbite sticks with us better because it is processed in our right brains—the creative side of the brain that processes information faster. Our right brain is the emotional side of our brain. When we make an emotional connection, it's more powerful. We're in alignment with the communication.

We can literally "see" how a concept works, as opposed to hearing it taught. In the case of abstract concepts, where there is no kinesthetic opportunity to experience the concept by "doing," as you might be in a lab or in the field, the graphic presentation appeals to the strongest potential absorption process we have. This is also why prototypes and demos move people more than slideshows.

Audiences, including your employees as well as your customers, are sold when they get your vision and accompanying visual representation of the future of your new product initiatives. Your focus, therefore, should be on making it easy to not only see but to experience your vision. To best achieve this, you need to create a new model for digital transformation buy-in such as creating a working prototype, building out a clickable website, even something as simple as a concept model.

Digital is meant to be a light technology—meaning it should be easy to create prototypes in various channels. Whether it's a design mock-up of a page or a clickable working prototype, you can get conceptual information in front of people quickly, and they, in turn, can absorb it faster. Building twenty manufacturing centers is a tough concept to prototype, but with digital, you can create clickable design mockups, cutaways and 3D renderings, and more. These tools convey the different aspects in a more holistic fashion. Prototypes can be anything from a quick sketch to a complex, proof of concept device that works. Implement rapid prototyping in the strategic planning process to iterate quickly rather than creating wordy PowerPoint files. This approach complements your strategy and accelerates buy-in. It doesn't have to follow the long-form agency process. This quick prototyping also keeps participants engaged and regularly participating in generating ideas for the initiative. Here are the basic steps most prototypes go through during a series of iterations:

Use Sketches

How many great ideas started out on a cocktail napkin? A lot. There's power in even the most humble of visuals. Sketches would be the lowest level of fidelity (how crisp and close to the design it is). Here a picture, even a concept drawn on a scrap of paper, can be worth a thousand words.

Create Design Mockups

Design mockups require using a designer to quickly pull together the core features and elements of the page. It's possible to make these elements clickable. Using a tool like Invision, for example, you can move a contact button from one side of the page to another. Static designs can be uploaded directly into Invision, and then you can create "hotspots" which transform them into an interactive and animated formats. Collaborators and customers can open the design on their devices, or you can use a live feature which is sharing enabled for group usage, like a virtual whiteboard.

Build Responsive HTML Prototypes

Creating a responsive HTML website means you're actually building the front-end of the website to the backend. You aren't creating the database, you're building in the tools viewers will use. Because mobile growth is outpacing, other forms of communication intake, for example, ensuring a gratifying, and intuitive experience for mobile users should be a priority. Responsive HTML provides a way to adapt the user experience in a fluid and positive way when change occurs in the way they're viewing your information.

Digital Demands Dynamic, Not Static Planning

Working off of a PowerPoint deck, with a static, linear plan is tediously slow and the end product is most likely to be stale once it hits your website, let alone social media. Alternatively a dynamic planning approach uses *iterations,* allowing you to adjust, adapt, and change your plan as you move forward and as events and circumstances change. This agile approach puts you ahead of, rather than behind your competitors. For instance, if Nabisco had stuck to a static plan during the 2015 Super Bowl, they'd never had been able to Tweet their now infamous line, "You can still dunk in the dark" after the Superbowl lights inexplicably went out. Dynamic planning allows you to take advantage of the world and events around you, but static does not.

Dynamic planning recognizes that the mode of delivery is such a critical element of the message itself. Reaching customer touchpoints to establish that all-important emotional bond, which in turn will lead to a buying decision, is the endpoint of a dynamic planning strategy.

Let Analytics Drive Your Strategy

Don't try to predetermine how your customers will react to your digital rollout. You can't foresee their reactions no matter how intuitive you think you are. It's better to just roll out your initiative and let the actual analytics tell you which way to go next or which was the right answer. There are a lot of low cost, low impact tools that can do this now. You don't need a laborious, very expensive design agency process.

Some organizations spend millions on traditional design agencies. We've seen companies we've worked with spend a million dollars to get two pages designed. There was very little business strategy rethink. The agencies they worked with are among the most talented design agencies around. In terms of visual presentation, they make some of the most beautiful websites on the planet. Their product is probably equivalent to the work of a couple of very talented designers, but they initiate a whole process wrapped around their design efforts. That process costs lots of money.

You may have the greatest design in the world but if what's missing is the business strategy, you've really got very little. Design is the very necessary after product. It's similar to picking the right technology. There are a lot of solutions, but you have to figure out the right strategy first.

The old game of the CTO/CIO blaming poor performance on lack of the proper technology went something like: "We don't have the right CMS," or "Our web interface isn't user friendly," or "I can't pull the data I really need." Unfortunately, this is still the case in some organizations, but most have figured out that analytics is really more of a strategic, top-down issue.

Much of the time, the motivations for these misappropriations lie in political positioning within the organization, or failure within a team framework. One large organization in the publishing space, for example, had a situation where the CTO regularly sent complaints about the creative team to the CEO who found herself a world of angst as a result, not the sort of things a CEO should be focused on. The CTO was doing this because he was jockeying for the spotlight, pushing to show how all his projects needed to be the first things anyone thought about.

Technology in a digital initiative is a means to an end. It is a tactical aspect that supports an organization's overall strategy. When there is a healthy organizational strategy that includes buy-in within the organization, it is a relatively easy matter to design and develop a digital strategy which promotes its objectives.

In the past, there were so many unknown factors in developing a quality digital team. But now, we are past the infant stage or even the adolescent stage of digital technology. Today's technology is much more sophisticated, and yet it's easy to find quality coders and designers. Instead of adapting to something new in the technology arena, it's much more about strategic challenges. The combination of business strategy with strategic thinking about the user experience is bigger than a site launch or a redesign.

Change flows from strategy to tactical tools. Today, business is about asking smart questions like, "How are we changing our business in anticipation of changes we can see coming?" and "How are we positioning our messaging to address the issues our customers are facing today? Figuring out how to implement these changes on a website or even a mobile app is very secondary to changing the business itself. Changes in the delivery system need to reflect the strategic decision making that arises from properly assessing conditions, functions, and processes in and by which the business operates.

However, when it comes to mobile, there still are questions such as, "Should we have apps or responsive websites or both?" and "If we have both what goes in an app versus what's in a responsive website?" and "If we have apps should we have one app with all of our features or an app for every feature?"

Companies and their executive teams can get really wound up in this kind of debate. Rather than creating a three-dimensional model of strategic transformation, they focus on managing individual business units who say they want to create an app, or a website, or some other digital asset. This hierarchical somersault can deviate drastically from any sort of overall strategic plan into a failure freefall.

Companies shouldn't even try to debate these issues among themselves at the executive level. The goal of the executive team here should be to define the experience of the future. Once that vision is defined, it is the job of the digital transformation leaders to determine how it is broken down into different websites and applications. Your task as a leader is to define the objectives. Their task is to translate that definition into specific digital experiences. Your task then becomes evaluating the information gained from the transformation as to whether it met the strategic objectives, and then to make applicable changes for the best result possible in alignment with those objectives.

When this sequential process is adopted, the implementation of the vision is actually the easier part. You already know how your audience is approaching you for information and purchasing from your research on touchpoints, use cases and journey mapping. This information will determine what should be in your app, what should be in your website, what should be part of your social media outreach.

Should a single audience only want to deal with certain features, while another only wants to deal with other features, your team designs with those preferences at the forefront. This is where strategic opportunities meet digital user experience. Again, the goal for those leading the digital transformation is to be able to identify their differentiation and *their* consumer experience, not the entire consumer experience. Each company needs to focus on their experience, their digital DNA, and what sets them apart, not on what the other is doing so they can copy it.

Action Steps

- Include your digital leader as a key participant in strategic business planning.
- Identify resources within your organization that could be permanently or as needed assembled to form a rapid prototyping team.

- Challenge your team to present their next strategy in a visual way without PowerPoint.

- Layer digital data points on your customer segmentation to understand where your users may be engaging with your brand.

- Journey map your top user experiences.

- Publish your strategy on a social collaboration/Wikipedia-type platform that allows other employees and even customers vote, comment, and contribute.

7

Roadmapping Your Digital Transformation

Your digital transformation is a journey. Journeys require maps. As aligning digital with the rest of the organization's strategies and activities is crucial to your success, nothing is going to be more important to the successful execution of your transformation than a well-documented digital roadmap.

Objectives of a Digital Roadmap

There are several critical objectives for digital roadmaps.

A Digital Roadmap Is Easily Accessible

Often companies will put together their roadmap and create their digital strategy but won't integrate it enterprisewide. It will be rolled out and receive a lot of attention the first week, then sit in people's email, forgotten, the rest of the year. A roadmap is not just a list of things to do, or a collection of data reports and a status update every 6 months. A great digital roadmap is a living and breathing entity. It is extremely important that you *do not* allow a digital roadmap to sit static, in the form of a file that only gets reviewed on occasion. Just like your strategy, a digital roadmap needs to come "off the page."

A Digital Roadmap Is Dynamic

Once this roadmap is created, it should reflect the fact that it is indeed a living, breathing, entity that interacts with your organization and vice versa. Over the course of it, you should see it shift, change, and morph as you continue to monitor, track, and adjust your progress along the way. The roadmap should tie your progress back into your updated strategies as you go, and employees should be able to monitor that all along the way. The roadmap should literally be published and available for everyone to see, comment on, and share.

It should not sit in a drawer or be forgotten a week after it's rolled out. One way to accomplish getting your roadmap off the page and bringing it to life is to apply social media concepts to the traditional business planning process. Give people the ability to like, vote, comment, and plug into your map. It should reflect your vision in an ongoing basis, as though it was alive and new every week. This roadmap should be a link, a viral and vital part of your company's day-to-day processes. No one in your organization, employee, contractor, or consultant, should be able to say "I don't know where we are or where we are going" on the company's digital journey.

A Digital Roadmap Is Social

Third, successful digital marketing roadmaps align your goals, strategies, and tactics in a clear and visible way. These goals, strategies, and tactics shouldn't be a secret to your employees. Everyone in the company needs to have access to the map and be able to comment, suggest, critique, and interact with it. That way, you're crowdsourcing great ideas, giving people across the organization the opportunity for buy-in, and keeping peo   ple plugged-in, so it's always in their face and demanding attention in a way that makes it better. It's not enough to know *where* you want to go. The most critical aspect of any transformation is that everyone in the company is onboard and following the organizational vision and roadmap. For instance, if you spend millions to develop a customer-centric business model that focuses on sterling levels of customer service, then fail to train the sales staff and customer service agents in customer service, your model will fail.

A Digital Roadmap Is Visual

Last, your roadmap should have multiple, powerful, and visual tools. This visual aspect is important because it helps people quickly align with where the roadmap is really starting from. These tools also give your employees several different perspectives about what's happening so they can actually engage with the transformation and socialize it internally, across the enterprise. Your roadmap shouldn't be just one document with one perspective. It should be multilayered and include multiple slices of a variety of kinds of data about the steps you'll be taking along the way. We can't say that enough, visual tools are critical for conveying your vision and creating a roadmap that works. Visual data trumps numbers, text, and two-dimensional data. Destinations on your map may include capabilities, product releases, phases of work getting completed, maturity levels being achieved, and implementing processes, and they should do so in a visual way, whether it's with graphs, photographs, video, or infographics. People should be able to tell at a glance where the company is on the map at any time. Visual tools, and why you should use them, all come back to aligning your digital transformation with everything else in your organization so that you realize the best success.

A Digital Roadmap Is Aligned to Business and Technology Roadmaps

You've looked at the strategy and visualized your journey. You see that the transformation is going to require a new website, and a new mobile app. Your site needs be fully responsive to be able to integrate with IoT (Internet of Things) sensors.

You see you will also need a whole new set of marketing capabilities. Additionally, other functions in your business will need improvements. All of a sudden you're talking about lots of features, lots of tools, lots of platforms, and you wonder which of your people are going to implement these changes? How are you going to create an organization to do this? It can become overwhelming if you haven't spent time drawing up the right map. Focus now on aligning your digital roadmap with business and IT changes.

Focus on one thing at a time rather than multitask your map. That one focus can be many things along or on the roadmap, but the point is to understand you've got one kind of map, not seven. Many companies have several maps that might overlap, but they're not aligned. They may have a consumer strategy and a digital strategy that overlap but are not aligned. Your business strategy and roadmap should contain digital at the center. You also need someone at the top leading the transformation. Then you develop a collaborative network of digitally adept participants inside and outside of your organization.

A Digital Roadmap Is Easy to Understand

Strategy needn't be that complex. Some of the business strategies we've heard leverage analogies like "The mint.com for health", referring to what Mint.com has done for financial services by putting the big picture of a customer's finances at their fingertips—so they know what they're earning, spending and investing in order to take advantage and control of their money. Imagine doing that with your health-care provider. Ultimately digital transformation will challenge to you change how you do *business*, meaning how your culture works, what your business model is, and how you connect and engage with your customers. It won't be easy, so there is no need to make the process more complicated than necessary.

Components of a Digital Roadmap

A roadmap typically shows phases of work or maturity levels you need to achieve in digital. Those can include the following:

Initiatives Are Organized by Release Dates

Both the passage and the dimension of time can easily be shown graphically. Write down what you anticipate will happen with your digital initiative, when these milestones will occur, what features and capabilities you will roll out at what time, and what a changing maturity or focus will look like and when it will occur. Small companies may make the change in months or years, while larger companies may be looking at a decade or more to achieve digital maturity. As cliche as it can sound, transformation truly is a journey. You need to make sure you're progressing consistently. This is where visual tools can help bridge gaps as well as alter the perception of time in ways that keep people engaged and focused. Setting a baseline, creating benchmarks that line up with your goals, will help you estimate how long your transformation will take.

Initiatives Are Grouped by Categories

Grouping things by category helps people see the big picture at the same time they're looking at the details.

Initiative Costs Are Represented

What is the cost of each item? Investing in a digital transformation shouldn't be done without considering what the investment is going to cost. Begin your journey by taking inventory. Compare your current inventory, including human resources, technology, culture, brand, sales force, marketing, and customer data to what you'll need to acquire along the way.

Initiative Complexity Is Represented

Beyond costs, some initiatives are more complex to roll out due to regulatory challenges, the number of areas within a company that are impacted by the initiative, and so on.

Initiative Impact Is Represented

What is the number of units impacted, and how, when, where, or why are they impacted? This is a great place to use visuals.

Prioritization of Initiatives and Features Is Represented

Sometimes it's important to breakdown the features of the road-map to determine what the various priorities are. For example, maybe you want to address a feature that has a high priority and high impact versus a low priority and low impact. Powerful visuals that convey this distinction can help participants align at a glance with your initiative.

The roadmap begins when you start your digital transformation. Your transformation begins with the creation of a vision communicated to the rest of the company. Support of the vision begins when you get buy-in both laterally and hierarchically in the organization with your roadmap. The value of your transformational initiative must be heard and taken seriously, and this is where a dynamic roadmap comes in. It anchors the vision. If the next steps that participants take are not in alignment with your vision, lack focus or veer off track, your transformation will derail.

Technology Represented as Enabling Business Capabilities

Understand and communicate that digital is much more than "an Information Technology upgrade." It's an all-encompassing business model and therefore must have a customer-centric focus from the inside out. Digital transformation is both the roadmap and the desti-nation. It may involve developing a variety of areas, but ultimately it's about enhancing the customer experience and the ways in which your constituents connect and engage with your company. To enhance and expand the experience, you've got to implement transformation from within—your people, processes, and tools will all undergo some varying levels of change. Businesses often worry about whether they'll have the technologies or the people or the process to make their transformation a success. Your roadmap needs to consider these elements across all of the business units of your enterprise. It should include technology releases, and factor in both current and future capabilities of the organization. For example, what tools you're putting in place, whether it's technology platforms, project management platforms, or making sure the people you have are in the right roles. Next, include the processes and individual tactics that comprise the action steps toward achieving the objectives. What is your baseline? What does digital transformation mean to you? Whatever technologies you choose make sure that you have ample support internally and externally to ease the transition you will be making from one system to the next.

Views of a Digital Roadmap

Quantifying Value

Companies continually struggle with figuring out the ROI of digital transformations. The fact that these initiatives have wide ranging impacts is one reason for the difficulty. For example, in the rapidly growing mobile app space, one Gartner study predicts that through 2016, 75 percent of mobile apps will be developed with little or no business cases to back their creation.[1]

Further, the technologies are evolving so rapidly that many companies have trouble assessing the long-term potential of certain investments. This is often the case in the 3D printing space or wearables, but of course can apply to many other digital spaces that are in a growth phase (Figure 7.1).

Prioritizing

The best strategy for launching a digital transformation becomes not assessing an initiative too early or too late. Give your initiatives

---

[1]Gartner, "Survey Analysis: CFOs' Top Imperatives from the 2013 Gartner FEI CFO Technology Study", May 2013

PRIORITY 1	MUST HAVE	TOTAL 3 YEARS BENEFIT	IT COST	ROI	AVERAGE QUALITATIVE RANK
Feature Group 1					
Feature A	●		$744,347	−100%	4.0
Feature Group 2					
Feature A	●		$97,627	−100%	3.3
Feature B	●	$137,988	$100,723	37%	3.0
Feature Group 3					
Feature A	●	$14,171	$17,200	−18%	4.3
Feature B	●		$80,496	−100%	3.7
Feature C	●	$451,360	$126,523	257%	3.5
Feature D	●		$186,654	−100%	4.5
Feature E	●	$180,609	$200,483	−10%	3.7
Feature F	●		$5,588,314	−100%	5.0
Feature G	●	$9,313,093	$175,990	5192%	4.2
Feature H	●	$1,338,004	$685,523	−74%	3.6
Feature I	●	$175,082	$53,802	−100%	3.8
Feature J	●		$275,578	−95%	3.7
Feature K	●	$334,184	$214,450	3069%	3.8
Feature L	●		$12,384	10704%	4.0
Feature M	●		$150,603	16%	3.3
Feature Group 4					
Feature A	●		$483,492	−31%	3.7
Feature B	●		$3,835,087	−74%	4.0
Feature Group 5					
Feature A	●		$29,859	−100%	2.7
Feature Group 6					
Feature A	●		$62,780	−100%	2.0
Feature B	●	$2,083,422	$1,226,628	70%	3.3
Feature Group 7					
Feature A	●	$525,245	$734,393	−28%	3.6
Feature B	●	$14,171	$357,975	−96%	3.6
Feature C	●	$247,414	$91,573	170%	3.5
		$22,814,400	$15,532,487	47%	

Figure 7.1 Quantifying value matrix

enough time to assess their potential. Note again that a digital transformation spreads risk throughout the whole organization if you have involved all your business units in your effort. Realize that by doing this, you are then able to minimize risks, allowing your initiatives to get the legs they need to take your organization to the next level of performance. Consider focusing, first, on initiatives that advance your operations or the customer experience as these will render the best returns.

Another way of prioritizing is to start with a pilot. For example test a number of digital initiatives that focused on things like mobile

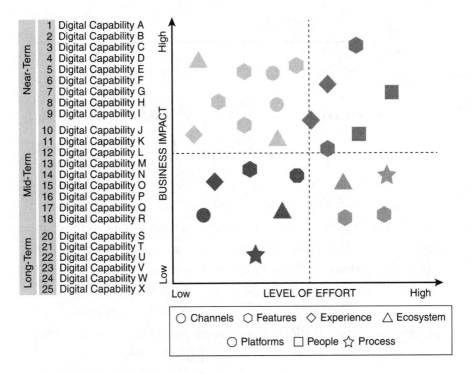

Figure 7.2 Prioritization visualization

and ecommerce. Tracking analytics assisted in decision making to refine the initiative (Figure 7.2).

Action Steps

- Mandate just one digital roadmap.
- Create a digital roadmap using a live tool that allows social media style interaction and permissions for all applicable participants.
- Create the forum to regularly review the digital roadmap with leaders outside of digital ensuring alignment.
- Align your digital roadmap to technology, business, and market-ing roadmaps.
- Get a budget view of all digital spend across the enterprise even if not managed by your digital team.
- Socialize the roadmap with all appropriate business units and divisions of the enterprise.

8

Organizational Capabilities to Drive Digital Transformation

Digital transformation requires both art and science to transform a traditional business model into a business model that can thrive in the digital age. We've seen companies try many different approaches to "get digital done" in their enterprise. The successful ones are those that are able to combine the right people (the art) with the right process and tools (the science). In this chapter, we'll outline how companies can structure their organizations and implement the right processes and tools to build and scale a digital business.

Before you can really discuss how to structure your organization, it's important to take a step back and understand your organization's roots, where senior management came from and who is a digital native and who is a digital immigrant. For instance, most people in executive management positions today were born before computers existed in the workplace. If they were exposed to computers, they entered the workforce before computers were mainstream, and they conducted business effectively without computers. On the flip side, anyone entering the workforce today doesn't know life or business without computers. It won't be much longer before the workforce won't have known a world before the iPhone or iPad. Until then, understanding who *gets* digital and who doesn't will be critical for any traditional business who wants to build or enhance their digital capabilities.

Back in 2001, Marc Prensky, an education writer, wrote an article entitled "Digital Natives, Digital Immigrants." The article dealt with the struggle of children raised in a digital, media-saturated world. To thrive and learn well, they required a media-rich learning environment to hold their attention. Prensky called these children "digital natives."

The metaphor was expanded to define "digital immigrants," meaning adults who were raised without digital technology, and who came to digital later in life. Like any immigrant in any new land, digital immigrants struggle with the "language," the culture, the etiquette, and the learning curve of digital. They must adopt a new way of thinking, relating and interacting with the natives. It's rarely easy and never quite like growing up a digital native. Some have more success than others obviously, but it's an important distinction to be aware of, particularly when it comes to the business world. In a business setting, the difference between digital natives and digital immigrants can cause conflicting ideologies, lack of understanding, communication issues around digital initiatives.

When there are natives and immigrants, there are conflicts around how people view information, how they prefer to communicate, and how they see relationships around people and institutions. The goal of a digital transformation is to learn how your customers find, explore, engage, communicate, and buy from your brand. For that reason alone it's critical for your employees to share, or at least understand, embrace, and leverage the different perspectives of digital natives and digital immigrants to end up with better overall decisions around digital.

Just as digital immigrant teachers struggle to teach digitally native students in a classroom, many traditional C-suite executives, most of them digital immigrants, struggle to understand the digital world and their digital native employees.

Choose the Right Digital Organization Model

Some of the fundamental questions companies have around digital within their organization include:

- Who "owns" digital?
- Where does digital sits in the organization?
- How does a digital team interact with other business units in the enterprise?
- Who "owns" the profit and loss (P&L) for digital business?

There is an argument that if most businesses have digital at the core of their business strategy, should there even be a separate digital division. In theory, once all employees at a company, including the C-suite are digital natives, the whole company should be operating the business by leveraging digital. How you structure your digital organization capabilities in your company should be correlated to how digitally mature the company is and how central digital is to its core business. The less digitally mature a company is the more it needs to centralize their digital efforts. Conversely, companies with a high level of digital maturity (e.g., Nike) the more digital may be decentralized. In digital native companies like Google or Amazon, digital is by default completely decentralized as the entire company is digital.

The diagram (Figure 8.1) provides a framework of common ways to structure digital organizational capabilities within a company depending on the digital maturity of the business.

Centralized Digital Team

Many traditional companies to date have created separate shared service groups within their organizations to own digital divisions. Sometimes they call their internal organization a "Digital Center of Excellence," a "digital" division or a "digital services group." "Centralized" means all the digital functions in the company are within this group and

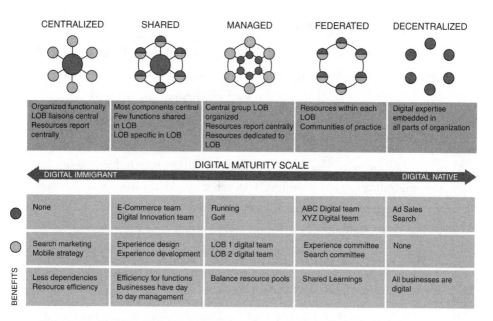

Figure 8.1 Digital organization models

the business units must work through this organization to get anything done in digital. The group is typically headed by a senior executive that reports to the Chief Executive Officer or up through a business side executive such a general manager or Chief Marketing Officer. More and more companies with this structure are giving the title of Chief Digital Officer to this position. This executive should be empowered with the decision authority, dedicated budget and resources to define and deliver whatever digital innovations and processes are needed.

Shared Digital Resources

In a shared model, business units choose to have their own team manage the digital functions most tied to the business, such as product management, ecommerce, digital marketing, digital strategy, and digital innovation. Digital functions that are more functional and agnostic to what the business is, such as user experience design, and front-end development, may be centralized in the shared service division.

Managed Digital Resources

In the "Managed" model, resources in all digital functions are separately dedicated to their respective lines of business, yet they are able to shift around their resources if not being fully utilized.

Federated Digital Resources

A federated model deploys digital resources into individual teams in each operating unit that are "federated" together usually by a committee structure or even sponsor executive to ensure they leverage best practices, standardize brand style guides, and more across business units.

Decentralized Digital Resources

Companies that have digital capabilities completely decentralized, or infused throughout the organization, are typically digitally native companies like Amazon or Google. Their entire business is digital, and hence there is no need for a centralized team.

Businesses often fail at digital because business units are usually fighting over who owns what in digital—who owns the P&L. Assessing your digital maturity and assigning a team structure will ensure a lot of the issues are eliminated before they become problems. A lot of companies have a concept of a shadow P&L where the digital team doesn't truly own the P&L, the business unit does. However, the digital team keeps what they call a shadow P&L. They are not focused on incremental revenue or cost, but rather a capture of the revenue and cost that's being driven by digital in one or many business units. Companies trying to digest this model, compared to creating a digital team that literally owns all the revenue coming out of the digital channel, makes it hard for companies because it's simply not a practical step for a lot of companies.

In between there are a number of various models. For example, at Federated they have digital teams in each business unit as well as a central team that's more of a center of excellence. Other organizations also have decentralized team structures where digital is housed completely in their business units. What we have found is that if digital is centralized in an organization, this represents the least mature model a company can create where digital is a separate, distinct business unit.

In this instance, these companies are typically creating digital divisions with the thinking that digital is a shared service that performs all their digital initiatives, and therefore, all their digital people should be clustered together there, doing everything the same way. Then there are organizations where one business unit has the biggest digital team and the other ones have smaller ones and they connect to the larger, core business unit.

As we said, how you structure digital in your company will have something to do with how digitally sophisticated your company currently is. How digitally sophisticated your company is doesn't mean how sophisticated your Chief Digital Officer is. It's more about the culture and how digitally sophisticated your people currently are. It also has something to do with how much digital currently plays a role in your business. For example, if your business involves digging natural resources out of mines, your digital structure may be different than if you're a retailer where digital is completely core to your operations and therefore should be at the center of your business. Digital in a natural resources company is an enabler of certain things, but it really doesn't have that much to do with the core business.

Ultimately figuring out what the right digital team structure for your company is becomes an important part of creating a digital team. Ask yourself whether your business needs a completely centralized team where the business units literally come to them like they would an IT department. Do you want company structure where people aren't allowed to touch technology or digital channels unless they go to the team in charge of digital? Or do you want to be more like a retailer, where you know you can't just centralize everything because there's going to be digital usage in the stores? How will you align the business so the people who run the stores are at least working closely with the digital team, or have a stake in their success so that the digital piece can thrive?

Establish a Digital Center of Excellence

It's one thing to lay out a strategy for your company's digital transformation, but if this change is really going to happen, you'll need a strong, structured team to lead the charge—in other words, a Digital Center of Excellence (DCoE).

To become a truly secure enterprise in today's business environment, building a website, mobile app, and social media presence isn't enough. Real digital leaders should be bridging the gap between physical and digital, leveraging digital capabilities in the physical world with wearables or smart devices. But before your company can become an industry leader, it needs to make wide-ranging transformations in several areas:

- Your organization and structure
- Your culture
- Your digital tools and technology
- Your focus on digital products from "must-have" features to the ideal customer experience

Completing these changes is the primary task of a DCoE. This department should be completely entrusted with your transformation, and be exclusively focused on digital operations. To give your company the speed and fluidity, it needs to compete with digital competitors. The DCoE must:

- Move your company away from a waterfall methodology toward an agile one, emphasizing adaptive planning and continual improvement of initiatives and products.
- Usurp the existing company culture with a new set of enduring assets. This strategy calls for the development of comprehensive

roadmaps and plans of action that keep your workflow dynamic rather than static, while also building teams of digital champions who act as resources for employees and spread ideas to lines of business and digital partners.

• Researching and purchasing the latest digital tools to enhance both production and internal operations.

Appoint a Chief Digital Officer

In 2012, Gartner predicted that 25 percent of companies would have Chief Digital Officers (CDO) by 2015; but by that time, less than a fifth of firms had or even planned to hire a CDO according to Forrester Research. Deloitte's 2015 Tech Trends Report claims that 37 percent of firms place responsibility for Digital Strategy at the "C" level, with an additional 44 percent looking to an SVP, EVP, or someone in a similar role to direct digital plans. This is a mistake, plain and simple. Now is the time for companies to rearrange their executive-level positions to make room for a qualified and imaginative CDO—before it's too late. Leaders in business and IT acknowledge the growing importance of a CDO and his or her responsibilities within a business. At the start of 2014, parroting boardroom conversations, Wired asked, "Is 2014 the Year of the Chief Digital Officer?" In November of 2014, TechCrunch came out with the similar assertion that "Every Company Needs a CDO." Author Neha Sampat of raw engineering explained how a CDO "can think holistically about how a company's strategy is executed across all digital channels—such as mobile, the Internet of Things (IoT), and an increasingly important SaaS-based web—and can provide insight and recommendations on how to reconcile the digital experience for key target audiences." The CDO plays the pivotal part of ensuring that all aspects of a business are represented digitally and integrated in a way that's efficient and effective. This is, without doubt, a huge responsibility.

Choosing the Right Candidate for CDO

Not just anyone can do this job, especially considering the fact this position didn't even exist 20 years ago. Many companies make the mistake of putting executives with little digital experience in the position of a CDO, therefore, placing a colossal amount of responsibility in the hands of someone who is inexperienced and unqualified for the role. Business knowledge doesn't necessarily equal digital know-how, and this distinction is one that companies must grapple with when rearranging or reallocating corporate responsibility.

A CDO requires more than just extensive knowledge of the digital world—he or she needs to design and execute a vision that integrates each and every digital aspect of a company or organization. Not just anyone has the know-how to ask the right questions, and a good CDO will urge a company and a brand to continue to push for digital innovation while bridging the gap between marketing and technology.

At this point, there are plenty of people who've spent their entire careers in the ecommerce divisions of brick and mortar retailers, but traditional companies have to make sure that employees like these don't get—or stay—complacent. Traditional organizations must challenge themselves to bring in new talent with strong backgrounds in digital, and they must set them up with the right organizational structures and incentives to disrupt the status quo.

Sharing Responsibilities with Similar Executive Roles

As the Chief Digital Officer is a relatively new role in the C-suite or C-level team, it's important to balance the responsibilities between this new role and the more traditional roles such as the CTO (Chief Technology Officer), the CIO (Chief Information Officer), the CMO (Chief Marketing Officer), and, the other CDO (Chief Data Officer). Each and every one of these roles will vary, of course, depending on the company's product and business model—and some larger firms may boast all five of these roles, while some may pack the responsibility into just two or three.

First, let's look at the CTO and the CIO. A CIO is the go-to commander and problem solver for a company's existing technologies, responsible for making sure the company is constantly adapting to new and necessary tech and IT products—software or hardware. The CTO's focus, on the other hand, is on identifying and implementing new technologies, and it's the more externally driven of the two roles—the CTO wants to make sure the customers and clients are on the receiving end of the highest-quality and most efficient technology possible. To completely oversimplify it, a CTO handles external operations and improvements, while a CIO's focus is largely internal.

On to the next and most easily differentiable role—the CMO. Often referred to as a company's informative "nexus," the CMO's responsibilities span from sales to product development to marketing, and even all the way to customer service. As this marketing-driven nexus, a CMO must work closely with other C-level employees to make sure that the marketing sector is utilizing the most up-to-date technologies and strategies to promote their product or brand to the world.

Chief Digital Officers and Chief Data Officers not only share an acronym, but some responsibilities. As you might expect, a data officer extracts and analyzes data to inform a company's business strategy—they must know how to gather information and, more importantly, they must know how to effectively use it to improve a business. The Chief Digital Officer, on the other hand, oversees data assets with a marketing- and technology-sensitive eye.

In many ways, a fruitful combination of the CIO, CTO, and CMO (and also, perhaps, their successor, according to Znet), a CDO's job is to constantly reshape a company's structure and strategies to ensure that it's taking advantage of any and every new technology or data-driven service. These slight differences in roles and responsibilities aside, keep in mind that most of these jobs are working toward a greater common goal—using technology and data to transform business. Although some positions are certainly more data driven while others are more geared toward marketing, the point is that companies are now increasingly allotting C-level roles to people who know how to seamlessly incorporate technology into a business' overall strategy and daily operations.

Define Standard Digital Team Roles

Companies can have various digital teams that can include digital strategy, digital marketing, and certainly digital products. The diagram (Figure 8.2) illustrates the various functions incorporated in these teams.

This completely specialized department will be made up of a number of teams and roles, each of which emphasize accountability for individual projects, initiatives, and products. Here are some of the typical functions within a digital center of excellence or team:

Example: Digital Strategy

More likely than not you will find that you need additional outside support to implement your digital initiative. Start looking for

DIGITAL CENTER OF EXCELLENCE					
DIGITAL STRATEGY	DIGITAL MARKETING	SOCIAL MEDIA	DIGITAL PRODUCT MANAGEMENT	DIGITAL DEVELOPMENT	PROGRAM MANAGEMENT OFFICE
ENTERPRISE STRATEGY	DIGITAL PLANNING	SOCIAL STRATEGY & MANAGEMENT	PRODUCT MANAGEMENT	SCRUM MASTER / PRODUCT OWNER	PLANNING & GOVERNANCE
EMERGING TECHNOLOGIES	SITE PERSONALIZATION	SOCIAL LISTENING	USER EXPERIENCE	FRONT-END DEVELOPMENT	PROJECT MANAGEMENT
BUSINESS UNIT STRATEGIES	MARKETING OPTIMIZATION	COMMUNITY MANAGEMENT	VISUAL DESIGN	CONTENT MANAGEMENT	RELEASE MANAGEMENT
EDUCATION & THOUGHT LEADERSHIP	SEARCH		PROTOTYPING	TESTING & QA	RESOURCE MANAGEMENT
ANALYTICS	CONTENT MARKETING		USABILITY		

Figure 8.2 Typical functions in digital teams

strategists who have not only expertise in your vertical but with a wide variety of verticals. The emphasis here should be on locating people with digital talent over vertical industry expertise.

Example: Product Management

Are all of your digital product managers ready to collaborate with one another to collectively implement your digital rollout? If not, find the time to get them together and on the same page.

Assess attitude as well as skill sets. Do you have a collaborative culture? Do your employees work well as part of a team? Are they able to dialogue, engage, and work things out? One of the challenges with digital is that people often spend more time with devices and less time on developing their skill sets around interaction—which can lead to a workforce where collaborative skills are often lacking, especially if you have a mixture of digital natives and digital immigrants. Take time to ensure that each group understands they have something to contribute to the mix. To ensure that the experience being designed is aligned with user needs, these managers take ownership of individual products and help development teams by becoming the voice of the customer. As the design teams try to bring business goals and requirements to life, product managers serve as experts on what users actually want from individual products. These employees are tasked with developing the user experience. They determine how customers should move and feel when they use your product or service, mapping out the individual journey they want individual users to take.

Example: Digital Operations

Representing the top level of management for the Digital Center of Excellence, this team exists to make sure everything, from products to content, is running efficiently and getting things done on time. Different members are tasked with different priorities like compliance, regulatory issues, planning, maintenance, finance, and quality assurance.

Build Digital Talent and Culture

Many companies feel like they keep swinging between outsourcing all their digital to hiring all functions internally. Thus they start by utilizing a variety of agencies and contractors, then shift gears and cut back on hiring to save money. During that shift, they may then bring everything in house. These constant shifts created in order to build their digital acumen, actually end up impeding their momentum. It's important to note that bringing things in house is not the same in digital as it may be in IT.

Digital transformation requires a mix of in-house and outsourced talent because of the different perspectives outside and internal digital teams can bring to your business. Not only do outside contractors live, breath, and work digital every day, they have a unique perspective on your company because they bring "new eyes" to your various opportunities and challenges. They also have a much wider awareness of what's trending in other industries that could be used in your strategy—digital applications that either aren't being utilized in your industry, or that no one has yet thought to utilize.

Digital is a very hot space to work in. Consequently, the very best people working in it want to do the most innovative projects, or they want to be challenged constantly, or they want to make a difference. They "do digital" because it's the world that is changing. It's not just about receiving a regular paycheck. It's more about a pathway. Digital stars, like the ones in demand by top companies want to learn, want to work with the best and the brightest, and want to be mentored to grow and continue to develop really amazing digital capabilities. They are driven by the opportunities to change the world, not just get a paycheck. They want to be part of something larger than their individual selves. They want to make a difference.

Don't think you can hire the best talent just because you offer a bigger paycheck. If you want brilliant digital stars, be prepared to compete with other companies to get their attention. Challenging projects, bleeding-edge opportunities, and a living and working environment on the east or west coasts are given if you hope to even get a digital talent to interview with you. That's why trying to cultivate this environment in an older, or more traditional company is going to be difficult.

If you're a traditional company not located near a coast, you can consider acquiring a *mix* of outsourced and insourced talent. This will allow you to bring in the top talent that wouldn't want to work for you directly on a full-time basis, but they might like the challenges of your projects mixed in with their other projects and clients. Sometimes finding a way to digitally transform a traditional company is more challenging and exciting if it's part of a mix of projects rather than a permanent position.

Another mistake companies make is trying to find people with digital experience and acumen in their industry, often thinking this will help them understand and work within the culture or the company. Traditional companies in your industry may not be good at digital to begin with. In addition, they likely bring the same ideas and thinking that's standard for the industry and possibly your company, limiting exposure to new ideas, strategies, and models. The whole point of bringing in outside talent is to bring new blood, concepts, experiences, and ideas to your transformation.

Rather than looking for someone or something familiar, search for people who have worked outside your industry. Look at other industries with similar functional attributes and operational complexities (e.g., a retail ecommerce or digital healthcare executive for a digital bank position). It's critical to recognize what roles are best suited for internal employees, as it requires a much greater connection to the business, versus what roles require more connection to outside the industry in order to gain a fresh perspective. For example, your digital strategy team should have its leader, and depending on your size, some core resources as internal employees. However, the digital team will also benefit from having an external strategic thinking partner or consultant that focuses on digital all day for multiple clients. This partner will be in a position where they can get fresh outside perspective on a regular basis. Alternatively, depending on your business and location, you may do better by outsourcing roles like user experience designers. These roles are more functionally aligned than business aligned. Plus, the type of talent that seeks out these roles may not thrive in a traditional company environment. They will bring more creativity and unique ideas to their work if they are working in multiple industries at the same time. The average traditional company will not be focused on how to cultivate a role like that. Therefore, consider outsourcing roles like this. On a role-by-role basis, determine if you are able to provide the infrastructure and acquire the talent to fully mentor and grow that talent.

Development and Training

What training do you need to implement to get everyone on the same page to proceed with your digital initiative? Again, different people are going to be in different phases of readiness. Bringing everyone up to one speed is a critical component of an implementation strategy.

Leveraging Global Talent Remotely

Outsourcing is nothing new. Since it has become a mainstream business practice, there have been many debates about the challenges and issues of companies based in the U.S. outsourcing technology work to countries such as India. Many companies outsource from a cost perspective; however, the savings is sometimes lost on the general communication issues of over the phone (which can be just as troubling locally), delay of work over different time zones, and lack of connection with the local team, and the cost of travel to improve engagement. While these are valid concerns, at least in the context of digital capabilities, working with remote teams deserve renewed consideration if you have already outsourced your work.

First of all, digital itself has brought great communication tools that help any remote teams stay connected and working collaboratively whether they are in the same building on different floors or in different contents. Internet-based video chat applications such as Google Hangouts and Skype are low cost or free, very easy to use, and are far more engaging than a telephone-based conference call. Couple this with other real-time collaboration tools (e.g., InVision for design, Trello for product backlogs, etc.) that can be used on digital projects, you can begin to see how you can address the issues previously reducing the advantages of leveraging remote teams. There are also many web-based marketplaces like UpWork which can help source talent all over the world, eliminating the need to establish local infrastructure before building teams.

Other things that have changed are the emergence of many areas of talent across the world and even the patterns of specialties that tend to favor one area or another. While India is certainly still a strong source of talent, both in numbers and technical ability, there are many other areas to integrate into your talent pool. Talent is global. There are countries known for certain areas of expertise, or who have a history of certain skills. For example, many companies have had tremendous success in Central and South America (e.g., Argentina, Columbia, Costa Rica, etc.) finding companies who specialize in design and front-end development. Eastern Europe (e.g., Hungary, Poland, etc.) are world renowned for software architecture and development talent.

Don't limit leveraging global teams to purely product development. Many companies are also leveraging global teams for digital business and marketing capabilities, such as analytics, lead generation, search engine optimization, social media management, and so on.

Compete for the Right Digital Talent

Being involved almost in any role in this digital boom time has talented tech people excited and looking for the best, most challenging companies and projects to work with. As a result, on the company side, it's getting harder and harder to find talent in certain geographical areas. For instance in the United States, the digital talent is centered in New York and San Francisco, and to some degree Austin. Why? Because digital talent works hard and plays hard. That's why they're attracted to the real kind of liberal, fun, exciting city areas usually found on the east or west coast. Chicago is in the midwest and is actually part of a huge digital hub, but there are organizations who have trouble finding talent here.

As digitally focused and expansive as the world is becoming, digital demand continues to exceed available digital talent. Enter the talent wars. Companies compete fiercely in the digital arena, boldly and brazenly poaching from each other's talent pools.

There are often agreements between some companies about not stealing each other's talent, yet talent is poached daily. Talent wars often focus on company versus company. Poaching and talent wars occur primarily on the east and west coasts, becoming the main challenge of larger, coastal companies. But what about the midwest, and companies located in rural or landlocked states?

How do companies attract people who would otherwise want to work at Google? Many traditional companies, and certain industries, need and want the best talent but they don't have the cache or the "sex" appeal a digitally native company has. So how do they compete?

Is it possible to attract the quality of digital talent that the digital native companies are attracting? Yes, it is, but only if you adopt, build, and then communicate to this digital native work force. You must convince the best talent, and that your company is committed to digital excellence, to digital transformation, etc. Offering young talent a chance at greater responsibility and a larger role than they might find on the west coast is one way to attract better talent. Making sure you understand what motivates them and how to communicate with them also helps.

Research continues to show that employees, particularly Millennials and Generation Z employees, aren't primarily motivated by money. Of course they like it, but it's not what drives them. Digital natives and digitally talented people are motivated by the chance to change the world and have an impact on the future of the people around them.

At first glance, a digital native may think your company is nowhere near the digital edge where they want to play. It's up to you to make sure that they know you are on a digital edge, or plan to be, with their help.

Traditional companies have to identify the unique capabilities, features, models, etc., that they could bring to the market that digital native companies can't. They have to show that they're committed to pursuing the cutting-edge digital initiatives that will attract the best of talent the current marketplace has to offer.

Establishing a Digital First Culture

As we've said, digital natives are literally born into a digital world. They don't know anything but digital; however, they often lack the context of digital and how it functions in the business world. Still, companies often feel they just can go out and hire a bunch of 25-year-olds and think it will solve all their problems. There's a reason so many traditional C-suite officers are middle aged—they have the real-world, real-time experience to put things into context. Young people are missing that business context and the communication and relationship skills of their older, digital immigrant co-workers.

Meanwhile, there are also legacy employees—people who weren't born before digital, but for whatever reasons aren't comfortable or well versed in digital. They're not as adaptive with it. So how can companies marry the two skill sets and train these very different groups? We think it's definitely something to explore.

Companies often don't know how to integrate the two parties. A lot of times we see the digital team is generally younger, and generally more digitally sophisticated, but they often lack the core business understanding of what the business is. As a result, the core business units brush them off. They try to minimize what they're working on. If and when companies figure out how to make those kinds of different viewpoints work together better, they really take it to the next level.

Cultivating Thought Leaders

Thought leaders can be found in engineers or other product designers who have visionary capabilities. In other words, people who can look beyond what they are working on now and both envision and promote new ideas and creations will become tomorrow's leaders. These leaders should also understand the agile process and iterative work. They should be open to digital development. In addition to the engineers or product designers in your organization, consider anyone in a position of influence within your company who has shown an openness to digital to be a potential thought leader.

Thought leaders can be made, so another option is to implement digital education programs across your organization and see who stands out, or quickly assimilates the teachings. These classes can look like live sessions through lunch-and-learn programs and/ or online sessions. They don't have to be long classes. Even hour-long sessions that share the details and benefits of the transformation can go a long way to develop support throughout your company as well as alert you to existing talent and potential in your current staff. Employees greatly benefit from this additional education. They are more likely to ask questions in a class environment where they're not expected to have all the answers, than in a work situation where they feel they may risk their job for asking about something they feel you may expect them to know already. Studies validate again and again the benefits of supplemental educational programs, so it only makes sense to host them.

Containing the Impact of Digital Resistors

So how do you address the concept of the "job jockey," digital disbelievers, and the usual assortment of micro-managers and bureaucrats? You find them their niche. For instance, we've come across companies that have built up their digital teams by taking people from other areas in their companies and pulled them into their digital teams with great success.

Yet, the companies we've worked with did it either because they didn't know what to do with these people, or the person had expressed an interest in digital yet didn't necessarily have the skill sets needed. These companies thought they could build a digital team better by pulling a people that "know their business." We're not saying everyone is cut out for digital, or that if you transfer the doubters and resistors into the heat of the kitchen they'll thrive. Many won't, but some will.

Success with finding the best slot for each employee goes back to a need for companies to have an understanding of digital acumen as a set of skills that are separate, but not necessarily equal to industry knowledge, experience, or acumen. For example, let's say that you are a great engineer who now has moved up in an engineering-focused organization like Motorola. You now have 2 years under your belt in marketing. You and your company believe that because you know your company's products like the back of your hand and you have some marketing experience, that you can confidently move up into a digital leadership role.

But will your skills translate well? Most likely they won't because you still need digital experience. This is where we continue to see companies making the mistake of trying to build their digital team from within their current employee ranks—let alone their marketing ranks.

For a variety of reasons, they're usually also scared to pick a leader for their executive digital team, meaning a Chief Digital Officer (CDO), from outside of their organization. Part of this reason is because an outside CDO won't know how to navigate the politics of their company. So, sometimes someone is chosen internally and made the CDO, but they're not really a digital person. As a result, we continue to meet people who are not skilled enough to manage or lead digital initiatives. Because of this, their entire company suffers and exposes itself to severe market-share erosion and financial decline.

Many companies have business units that don't necessarily discount that digital is important, but they do discount how important certain *elements* of it are for their business. They fail to imagine the impact digital now has on everything they do. So then part of the problem is that the digital team comes to them and says something like, "We've got to be on Facebook because everybody is on Facebook."

Digital resistors may think social media is only for younger generations. Here they're both wrong. First of all, the fastest-growing segment going into social media is an older, retired demographic. Part of the phenomenon there is that this is where all the digital natives or as we call them "new generations," also are today.

They are busy daily posting pictures of their growing kids. So that's where their parents, who are now grandparents, go to see their grandkids. That's a large part of what has driven so many new people into the digital world.

Meanwhile, the other mistake they're making is that they are overlooking the fact that this is just how a traditional company may need to leverage those channels.

The answer isn't always to get a Facebook page and get all your customers to like you. Instead, the answer to your challenges may lie more in the data that's on these networks. It's up to you to tap into this data to figure out how you can use it to make better decisions about what your customers want.

From this knowledge, you can learn how to develop the best lead-generation initiatives and so on. Part of the trick here is to find people who can put digital in context for traditional business units. This is the only way to get around the digital disbelievers. You can't just pull employees from across your organization into the digital team. Rather you have to find those people who understand the different digital landscapes and who know how to translate digital for traditional business units.

Implement Enterprise-Wide Digital Governance Processes

Implementing efficient, effective, and agile business processes around digital is critical to ensuring digital transformation initiatives. It's important that processes in general run the business activities and maintain support within a company and achieve business objectives. In a digital culture having committees or teams that create, implement, and enforce specific processes around digital is important, but those processes shouldn't be set in stone. The kind and size of committee or team you need to have for creating processes depends on the size of your company and how many digital issues you have or anticipate having.

Digital Budget Approvals

Sometimes money for digital comes from multiple areas, so it is often spent on duplicate areas. Having a committee that makes sure money isn't being spent redundantly, that there is no bad or inefficient spending going on becomes very important. This committee can check to make sure the right investments are being made, that opportunities to pool funds from different areas to make larger investments are weighed and that initiates aren't overlapping in nonproductive ways. This committee can also ensure the company is getting an economy of scale from vendors and agencies.

Digital Roadmap Prioritization

In larger companies, there are going to be multiple business units coming to your digital officer and saying, "I need this or I need that." You need some sort of prioritization process so the squeaky wheel isn't the primary determining criteria for awarding digital funding. If there are only so many people working on digital processes, who gets to say what's the higher priority? Too many companies want to hold prioritization process once a year. But by the time they schedule it and award it, the trends they're looking at have moved on. Prioritization needs to be a regular process, either weekly, monthly, or quarterly depending on your size and industry.

The reality of business is that while budgets may be annual, companies need to allocate a certain amount of money that's available to digital without locking down exactly what that money is to be used for. Have a more agile approach to prioritization and backlogging. The whole reason behind an agile approach is that you don't necessarily know the end result until you get there. You iterate as you proceed. You want to be able to be move, to be flexible, limber, and responsive to trends and opportunities as they arise. Coming up with a prioritization process that is constantly revisiting what the company's priorities are as availability of resources comes up monthly or quarterly is important.

Digital Strategic Planning

Strategy shouldn't be locked down or etched in stone. The framework can be permanent, but the details of the strategy should take into account new market forces on a regular basis. That doesn't mean the strategy changes every month or every 6 months. It just means that it's revisited, repeatedly discussed, and refined so opportunities aren't missed or overlooked.

Digital Results Measurement

There should be a constant assessment or monitoring, as well as consistent measuring and communication of the results of your digital strategies.

This doesn't necessarily have to be a meeting, but it should be a regular report that's sent out. It could be a webinar or conference call, but there should be some kind of regular reporting similar to how your sales reporting, or supply-chain reporting in traditional business is done. There should be regular digital reporting as well.

The basics, like traffic to the site, bounce rates, and social media metrics are important; but it's more than just reporting a bunch of numbers. This kind of reporting is about providing insights. A dashboard with the most important information available will let you do this. Dashboard the most important KPIs so you can get insights into what the most important numbers mean. Track the improvement generated by new implementations or new things you should do in digital.

Digital Program Communication

Getting companywide buy-in is critical to success. Here, get buy-in across as many groups in your organization as possible. You'll need a good communication plan so your transformation doesn't lose momentum. Executive buy-in is even more important than employee buy-in. Employees will follow the executive's example and lead. Use communication tools, such as newsletters, town halls, even drop-in meetings with internal influencers throughout your company. Good champions of communication would be employees with some form of digital backgrounds or those who you know would embrace digital transformation. Additional champions could be those who understand politics and/or those who have impact with both the C-suite and other employees. Also, look for others who have good PR (public relations) skills.

Champions include those in your organization who really understand the politics of the company. They should know and have influence with other key players in the organization. These people don't understand the landscape of the company, they understand how to best navigate it safely and effectively. Sometimes these strategists will overthink every little detail of something that somebody else may interpret as not such a big deal. A thought leader could be kind of obsessive about the details. Initiatives are sometime lost, not on their failure to deliver, but on their failure to keep people engaged. Additionally, if an initiative drags out too long, people become disengaged.

A top champion is also going to be the person in your organization who has accountability for improving the digital P&L of the business. Sometimes that could be a Chief Marketing Officer, or a Chief Consumer Officer. Sometimes champions could be the heads of divisions or business units or anyone who has the accountability for the digital P&L.

Ideally your best champion will be someone who is a natural leader and easily inspires other people. They should be someone who is a bit of a maverick and not afraid to take calculated risks and stick their neck out. Champions aren't just inspiring. They're also persistent, extremely hardworking, and dedicated to a passion and a goal. These are the most desired traits an individual needs to have to invoke change, yet they're less common than you'd think. In other words, leaders with all or even most of these traits aren't found in the 80 percent of most leaders; they're in the 20 percentile.

Communicating plans in any size organization, but especially the larger ones, is a vital touchpoint for any company. If you're going to improve the way your organization functions, you have to effectively and efficiently communicate the things you're doing, planning, or preparing to do. We touched upon this earlier when we talked about how quickly a small organization can change versus large organizations.

Large organizations aren't going to instantly become a 9-out-of-10 on the scale of digital transformation after reading a few books, or going to a seminar. Even working with a company who does the heavy lifting of the transformation for them won't magically transform them overnight. However, progress can be made. One of the keys to making progress is getting buy-in across as many key groups in the organization as possible and that means creating a good communication plan. This means, as we like to say in consulting, *socializing the plan*. With any kind of large, multiyear transformation initiative, you've got to have a good communication plan that doesn't lose momentum to ensure projects are kept on track. You also have to have executive buy-in and participation, persistence, and consistency. It takes time. And by time, we mean 3 to 5 or even 10 years. Smaller companies are looking at a minimum of 2 to 5 years. Understanding that it takes time and letting your employees know this is an important part of changing the culture so people embrace it, not dread it.

Action Steps

- Partner with external experts who can help you get to the next level around digital excellence.
- Commit to finding the right digital talent and don't just look internally to find true digital acumen needed to compete effectively.
- Search for people who can put digital in context for traditional business units.
- Determine the right digital structure for your organization.
- Assess your talent, tools, and processes on a regular basis to ensure you have the best mix possible to stay competitive.

9

Why Agile Transformation Is Critical to Achieving Digital Transformation

Given the pace at which digital is still evolving, in order to successfully execute a digital transformation roadmap, you're going to need an organization that is adapted to working in an agile framework. Many companies right now are starting to execute agile transformation initiatives. While some of these efforts are focused on software development, the reality is the spirit of "agile" software development could be applied to many, if not all functions in business. The most successful businesses today take iterative steps to all of their business processes, including strategies, design, and product development, making each iterative. While many companies and executive say they are agile or want to be agile, they need to recognize this isn't just something for their technology department to do. They need to acknowledge and implement a change in philosophy and culture. They need to understand where and how the business needs to do their part to operate in an agile way. The purpose of this chapter isn't to replicate what is already out there or provide a step-by-step guide of how to implement agile or execute the details of the agile project. There are plenty of great books and other content on the details of agile methodologies and how to implement them. Instead the goal, here is to provide business executives with a high-level overview of the key concepts within agile methodologies to be aware of as well as understand how to operate in this new framework.

Agile Benefits Over Traditional Methodologies

Companies think they're doing agile because they confuse "agile" with the *definition* of the word itself, and not with the *process* of agile. They think that agile means something gets done faster, or "we do less work to get to the same result." That can happen, but the reality is agile is more about a *process* to quickly create, release, test, get feedback, and improve that creation as you continue moving forward.

Rather than waiting a year to see the results of your project, you see it in one- to two-month intervals as it's created, not after it's created. With agile you're not waiting a year for a project to launch, then having to go back in and change or rework parts of it over the next year.

By releasing work at specific intervals, usually 2 to 6 weeks apart, you're able to see, shape, and test your project in a series of intervals called "iterations." You build as you go, repeating rounds of analysis or operations and making changes in each round until you are satisfied with the results. Writing this book, for instance, was an iterative process. It involved creating a proposal, along with an outline, then writing the first chapter, then another chapter, then comparing them to the original outline. As each chapter was written, the outline was tweaked so it reflected our vision better and so on.

Agile adapts management methodologies from agile software development (and agile project management) and applies them to project development teams. That's agile in a nutshell. It's a powerful way of managing people, teams, and projects, but it's more than that. It truly is a movement. Because the entire agile revolution was about a set of values rather than a process, it has the potential to create teams of empowered individuals, not just achievable deadlines and great products. The official agile manifesto is:

- Individuals and interactions over processes and tools
- Working software over comprehensive documentation
- Customer collaboration over contract negotiation

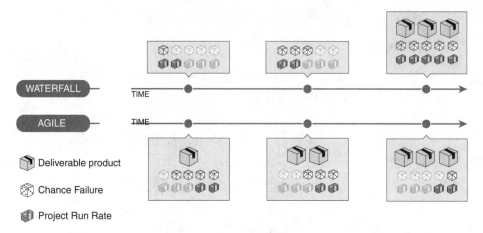

WATERFALL

AGILE

Deliverable product

Chance Failure

Project Run Rate

Figure 9.1 Benefits of agile over waterfall methodologies

- Responding to change over following a plan
- Real-time decision making and data-driven insights

Agile involves people working on the highest priorities of the business with a shared sense of purpose. When agile is done well, people and teams have fun and do great things. No wonder companies that do agile well love it.

Everyone has their personal reasons why agile is critical to a digital transformation, but the reasons we believe it drives value include the following.

Agile Gives Your Company/Team Real Feedback from Real People in Real Time

As we shared in Chapter 6, for most practical purposes, Power-Point is dead. It's dead because it's one-way communication—from the expert with the clicker in his hand, to the audience. There's no room for feedback from the audience unless the presenter is taking questions during the presentation. There's even less feedback from real customers about what the presentation is about.

Agile, however, gets you that real-time feedback. It helps you build the right product, service, or experience based on that feedback from real customers in real time. Instead of focus group(s) imagining what they might think, feel, say, or do with your product, you get actual data about how customers actually think, act, and respond— again, all in real time.

Faster Time to Market with Greater Predictability.

Speed matters, but predictability matters more. Development shops, vendors, consultants, and third-party partners will eventually "get it done," but it's almost impossible to find one who can get it done predictably. Agile creates a culture where people get good at making and meeting commitments and stabilizing their velocity over time. If you can't do B and C until A is finished, it doesn't matter how fast everything else gets done. You need to know exactly when A will be complete. Predictability matters more than speed because it's predictability that allows your teams to coordinate and align the other parts of the project, the strategy, and the business.

Agile Produces a Better Quality

The only thing people hate more than buying junk is working for a company that makes it. Making beautifully designed products that are also innovative is one of the reasons people love working for Apple. Apple epitomizes the tenets of the agile manifesto.

Agile provides the tools and the processes that allow companies to make a better quality whatever it is they make. Agile means better cars, better software, better customer shopping experiences, and better theme parks, among other things. Because agile allows teams to make better products, teams feel better about their products and so, in turn, they're inspired to keep improving, to keep innovating and to keep seeking excellence in their products. It turns into a win-win all the way around, from consumer to company to employees.

Agile Gives You Early ROI and Early Risk Reduction

What's the risk and what's the benefit to your company when you invest in some resource—whether it's technology, people, capital, or software? A high return on investment (ROI) means the investment gains compare favorably to investment cost, which is what you want, but can rarely guarantee—unless you have an agile system. Agile gives you early ROI and early risk reduction because it doesn't treat risk as a separate area that needs managing. Agile *is* risk management.

When you deliver early and get feedback at the front end of a project, you reduce the risk of building the wrong product. By focusing on architectural risk in the early sprints, you reduce the risk that you won't have a solution that can be built in time ... at least you'll know it early on. By continuously integrating and building defect-free software, you reduce the risk that your product wasn't built right just before you need to bring it to market.

Agile Is Efficient

Business is often still silo driven—meaning it can be mostly inefficient in many areas. It's even more inefficient when silo mentality sets in and people start hiding information from other silos, or competing with each other in unhealthy ways. In this case, people know that their existing business model, strategies, and silos aren't working well together. They know they spend more time in documenting, shuffling, and passing around reports and things that don't matter than they do just doing the work.

Agile eliminates redundancies and helps you become more efficient and productive, which means you can better able to scale, flex with daily demands and adapt, thrive, and grow. Agile also eliminates the things that clog up, slow down, or create backlogs, jams, missed deadlines, and inefficiencies. It empowers companies and their employees to get down to the business of creating new products that amaze and change the world.

Leverage Common Agile Concepts

There are actually many different agile methodologies. You may have heard terms such as adaptive software development, agile unified process, extreme programming, lean software development, kanban, Scrum. At their core, most agile methodologies have variations of the common concepts that we will generalize and define for the business executive in the following paragraphs:

Sprints or Iterations

Sprints or iterations incorporate the agile approach, dividing up work on projects into repetitive cycles called "sprints." Iterations chunk the work into more manageable pieces. These pieces are completed and reviewed on an ongoing basis, allowing for continuous improvement as the project moves forward. These iterations occur usually in two- to three-week cycles but can be shortened or lengthened based on the decision of the teams involved or the complexity of the project. Not every sprint will yield results that are ready for the end user. However, every iteration delivers something for leadership to review that shows incremental progress toward objectives of the project. These shorter iterations allow teams to receive ongoing feedback so that any changes or rework can be done preventing any project derailments.

Product Owner

The product owner is the project's key stakeholder. This is usually someone from marketing or product management. There can also be product owners that extend to other stakeholders or which include other leaders within the organization who funded the project and/or end users.

Scrum Team

A typical Scrum team has between 5 and 9 people, but Scrum projects can easily scale into the hundreds. However, Scrum can easily be used by one-person teams and often is. A Scrum team does not include any of the traditional software engineering roles such as programmer, designer, tester, or architect. Everyone on the project works together to complete the set of work they have collectively committed to complete within a sprint. Scrum teams develop a deep form of camaraderie and a feeling that "we're all in this together."

ScrumMaster or Project Manager

The ScrumMaster is responsible for making sure the team is as productive as possible. The ScrumMaster does this by helping the team use the Scrum process, by removing impediments to progress, by protecting the team from outside forces, and so on.

Product Backlog

The backlog consists of a prioritized list of features of all requirements or changes to a product initiative. Sometimes this can also include a sprint backlog that tracks the list of tasks to be completed during an iteration.

Sprint Planning Meeting

At the start of each sprint, the team involved holds an initial planning session. During this meeting, the product owner presents the top items on the product backlog to the team. The Scrum team selects the work they can complete during the coming sprint. That work is then moved from the product backlog to a sprint backlog, which is the list of tasks needed to complete the product backlog items the team has committed to complete in the sprint.

Daily Scrum or Standups

During a sprint or iteration, project teams hold daily 15- to 30-minute meetings to set the context for each day's work. These daily sessions keep the team on track and motivated. All team members must be present.

Sprint Review Meeting

At the end of each sprint, the team meets to demonstrate the completed functionality of their digital initiative. During this meeting, they demonstrate the new features of the initiative without PowerPoint slides.

Sprint Retrospective

Also at the end of each sprint, the team gathers to conduct a sprint retrospective. This is a team review session where the ScrumMaster, product owner, and team assess how effective Scrum has been working and any changes or additions they choose to make for it to work even better.

Codeathons and Hackathons

Twitter was originally a hack. People didn't get together to form a new business, raise capital, and pursue a business plan. It was invented at a hackathon in 2006 by a group of developers who wanted to test sending standard text messages to multiple users simultaneously. Hackathons are typically events over a day or multiple days where a group of designers and developers take an idea from concept to functioning prototype. They may work around the clock or have sleep breaks but never leave the room until the prototype is complete. It forces the team to breakdown unnecessary roadblocks to innovation.

Leverage Agile Tools

"Agile" methodologies changed the game in software development. With each successive gaming success, they started to creep upstream into product design, and later even into strategy and marketing. Now the heavy product management and project management processes and tools are also being replaced with agile. Forward-thinking teams are using a new league of lightweight tools that follow the 80/20 rule. They're focusing only on features that are really necessary and making them very intuitive. Where possible they're also automating the administration.

The point here isn't to give a detailed list of every tool you should be using, or to review all the tools out there. There are hundreds of apps and platforms your organization could consider to run its digital business. In the following sections, we'll outline the types of tools your teams should consider. Despite digital moving quickly where new tools are launched regularly, we'll even mention some examples of today's tools, at the risk of being outdated by the publishing date of this book.

Gantt charts are still powerhouses when it comes to project management. If you want a Gantt project plan, we've found the spreadsheet-like nature of Smartsheet as an easy program to learn, highly visual, and a real-time collaborative alternative to heavy enterprise systems. Consider Jira for development backlogs and combine it with Trello for more upstream business side product and project management. Many teams that used to seek out the activity feed of a platform like Basecamp have graduated to a more activity feed format like Slack.

Action Steps

- Identify champions in organization to support change.
- Create a communication plan.
- Establish an agile champion on the leadership team.
- Roll out educational programs to build support.

Epilogue

Examples of Digital Trends
Accelerating the Digital Revolution

There are a number of great science fiction authors who always write, quite accurately, about the future of technology, decades—or even centuries—before it appeared. Call them visionaries or modern-day prophets, but they have an eerie knack for envisioning the future of technology. They've done a remarkable job of predicting where the Internet and various technologies are going to go.

Jules Verne may have missed the total picture when he wrote about ships being shot out of cannons going to the moon but he was writing about space travel in 1865. Then there was Isaac Asimov who is credited with introducing the word "robotics" into the English language. He served as a scientific consultant for "Star Trek" and was sought after by the U.S. Defense Advanced Research Projects Agency (DARPA), which he refused to work with for fear that his work with them would be restricted under a governmental secrecy clause that would forgo his being able to write his science fiction stories. Next, consider Rudyard Kipling's 1905 short story, "With the Night Mail," was written only 2 years after the Wright Brothers succeeded in their first short flight, yet Kipling's story described airplanes delivering packages around the world.

Finally, there is Neal Stephenson whose books envisioned a world where everyone was coexisting vis-á-vis avatars in a digital world. His 1995 novel, *"The Diamond Age: or A Young Lady's Illustrated Primer"*, introduced many of today's real-world technological discoveries. The novel introduced extensive modern technologies, from robotics, cybernetics, and cyber cities to weapons implanted in characters' skulls. His next novel, *Cryptonomicon*, written in 1999, focused on codebreaking and cryptography as well as a data haven—something we call "the cloud"—15 years later.

Whether you look to science fiction, or follow the futuristic practices of the gaming industry, or any of the dozens of trendspotting websites, like trendhunter.com, it is possible to catch a glimpse of the future, or a strong probability of what the future could become.

We already know, based on the past, that digital as it continues to evolve will eliminate, redefine, and even do away with some existing jobs. At the same time, these revolutionary changes brought about by digital technology will create more jobs, and better paying opportunities across the employment strata. Just as Henry Ford's cars ultimately eliminated the existing demand for stable hands, it created new jobs for mechanics, engineers, and repairmen. We are better able to predict the future than the great science fiction authors of our time, but, we are eager to share with you the top ten trends we see emerging over the next decade. Paying close attention to these trends will help your organization get ahead of the curve to realize the benefits of early adoption when you apply them to digital endeavors.

Industrial Internet of Things

The Internet of Things (IoT) refers to the opportunity for many physical machines to have a digital identity to interact automatically with other machines. Similar to a social network, each machine's identity is like a profile or account that allows it to communicate with other profiles on the network, sending and resending data to one another. These clusters of communicating devices pool data that can be accessed and analyzed by humans, providing insights on different locations or systems that we otherwise wouldn't have accessed to. As these objects grow in number and purpose, the global network of objects communicating with one another will be able to pull in even more information at ever-greater speed. IoT technology currently has immense potential for businesses.

Known as "smart factories," industrial centers of production are using the IoT to manage factory activity. Through the use of purely machine-to-machine communication, and requiring no human intervention, these networks of objects collect and analyze data about factory activity and automatically make changes to maximize efficiency. The systems identify "dead time" and change the order or duration of certain aspects of the production process, prevent raw materials from being wasted, and detect product bugs before they're reproduced. In short, they change in the way that factories behave and manufacture.

For example, the rise of wearable technologies like the Apple Watch represents the IoT's best opportunity to access data directly from consumers. A device that's strapped directly to a person's wrist should be able to track his or her needs in a way that's more efficient than devices like smartphones or tablets, just by virtue of the fact that the device is always within reach. What's more, these devices could be tracking information that's literally vital: a user's heart rate. With companies like Fitbit offering watches that track your heart's BPM, your location, and the number of steps you've taken in a day, there are some pretty exciting implications for what wearables and the IoT could do for the healthcare industry. Giving whole networks access to data like this could alert physicians when their patients have a pending heart attack or stroke, for example, ensuring that they'll never be alone if disaster strikes.

For retail businesses, the IoT's potential value is in minimizing risk. If you're operating a brick and mortar location, machine-to-machine communication can do that by systemizing every aspect of the sales process and collecting data that could be used to improve them. For example, a company like Payless could place a digital signature on each pair of shoes it sells that's only activated if the pur-chaser returns it. This gives Payless more information about what shoes people are returning and why, thus helping them reduce the risk of more returns in the future. But this also applies to strictly online retailers. A company like Amazon might use it to add value to the supply chain by monitoring data storage warehouses. If their systems' capacities are being pushed to the limit and overheating, sensors in those warehouses could be automatically alerted. Those temperature sensors could then activate the facility's fans, keeping the processors cool and ensuring that the company's services don't crash at vital moments.

A new generation of sensors that can measure moisture in the air gives Southwest's airline better data than the U.S. government's twice-a-day weather balloon system. While dozens of other airlines were canceling Thanksgiving flights based on the U.S. government's weather reports one year, Southwest kept their planes flying. Based on readings from 87 of their sensor equipped planes, Southwest's chief meteorologist said conditions were too warm to produce the ice storms the government service was predicting. Southwest was right. Late flights cost airlines as much as $8 billion a year, so every advan-tage counts.[1] Sensors are now saving airlines millions of dollars in detecting the need, or not, to de-ice planes, or to ground or fly them based on weather conditions.

While most companies today are still struggling to understand and implement digital transformation, companies that are already well on their way to digital maturity will be light years ahead of their non-digital competitors once they implement IoT into their strategies. As big as consumer IoT (connected cars, smart homes, wearables, etc.) is, the Industrial Internet of Things (IIoT) will create new and more complex jobs and industries, and ultimately dwarf the consumer side

---

[1] http://www.bloomberg.com/news/articles/2014-06-19/airliners-become-weathermen-as-sensors-upend-forecasting

of business with its socioeconomic impacts.[2] The number of sensors (a critical part of IoT) shipped has increased more than five times from 4.2 billion in 2012 to 23.6 billion in 2014,[3] signaling the changes about to occur. The IIoT could impact more businesses than the Industrial Revolution, dramatically altering every possible sector of the economy, from manufacturing, energy, transportation, and agriculture to every niche of the current industrial sector.[4] You might be using some aspects of the IoT today, but is it providing you all the value it could be? Is your value chain prepared for the massive shifts that the IoT will bring to the world of digital service?

IoT also extends to pay-per-use models. For example, we could see insurance companies creating apps that allow drivers to purchase pay-as-you drive insurance for their automobiles.[5]

Big Data Visualization

Most traditional enterprises share a routine problem: They're sitting on more data than they know what to do with it. Today practically every organization's daily business activities are tracked and recorded digitally, meaning that there are millions of raw figures associated with every layer of its value chain. As useful as it may be, the sheer volume of relevant data makes it hard to work with.

Big data visualization helps you effectively communicate your most important findings so that your executives and customers spend less time trying to piece together the big picture and more time deriving insights and taking action.

---

[2] http://www3.weforum.org/docs/WEFUSA_IndustrialInternet_Report2015 .pdf

[3] http://blogs.cisco.com/ioe/the-internet-of-things-capturing-the-accelerated -opportunity

[4] https://www.accenture.com/us-en/technology-labs-insight-industrial-internet -of-things.aspx

[5] http://www.gartner.com/newsroom/id/2867917

The goal with big data visualization is to integrate it into analytics tools. This will enable multiple users to better interpret the data. It will also give them better predictive capabilities. Tools can include social media, videos, and so on.[6] The challenge will be to make these simple, self-service tools that can be used whenever needed.

Additionally, data visualization done well with customers will foster a more intimate business-consumer relationship. The more digital engagement you foster, the more you can learn about your, creating a feedback loop that will continue to inform your strategies for both content marketing and data analytics.

Future trends in this area will look like real-time, app-centric reporting that enables users to make better decisions faster.

Universal Streaming Media

Customers are gravitating toward streaming (renting) everything content related. People are moving toward a life in which they have no use for bookshelves or media storage (DVDs, CDs). People are truly cutting the cable cord in favor of direct-to-content producer services that are streaming subscription based.

Streaming media has impacted more than one company and more than one industry in the last decade—proving to be the powerful lever Netflix used to unseat Blockbusters, and that Spotify and other streaming music services provide as an alternative to downloadable music.

Having transformed the music industry once, with iTunes, Apple recently launched streaming music service, Apple Music, will attempt to differentiate itself from Spotify and other services by having playlists chosen by people rather than algorithms and technology that makes it easier to search for songs. Apple's not one to let unknown music makers escape. They'll also be following SoundCloud's lead,

---

[6] http://www.slideshare.net/HorizonWatching/data-visualization-horizon-watch
-2015-trend-report-client-version-28jan2015

seeking out unsigned acts in order to promote their music to music-lovers. The new, 24-hour radio station, "Beats One," is hoping to attract its already huge fan base to yet one more big Apple service.[7]

Meanwhile, Hulu.com has changed how people watch the television, Netflix streaming has changed how people "rent" movies, Kindle Unlimited is changing how people "take out" books from the library, Google has changed how people "pick up" the news.

Virtual Care

Call it Telemedicine, or virtual healthcare, but smartphone apps and the Internet are changing the way people seek medical services, diagnosis, and advice. Why wait to go to your doctor when your smartphone can help diagnose you in the privacy and comfort of your own home?

Having chest pain? The Heartcheck Pen, a handheld device which monitors heart rhythm and sends the results to your doctor for analysis, is now available for heart patients. Physicians must still interpret the results, but the Heartcheck Pen is the first of many more devices to come that will be able to monitor more heart and health conditions outside of a medical setting and send real-time results to your doctor's office.

Telemedicine is already using high-tech cameras and diagnostic devices to connect with patients in rural areas, or to allow people traveling around the country or the world to phone home to their own doctors.

Smartphones and other appropriate apps and devices have already been cleared to monitor and diagnose a variety of health conditions from thyroid disorders to Malaria. Researchers in Jamaica are already using embedded sensors in smartphones to detect early symptoms of exercise-induced asthma—eliminating the need for external

---

[7] http://www.economist.com/news/business/21654090-having-transformed-music-business-once-apple-trying-do-so-again-second-revolution #4j7huq73BXKv3fDW.99

monitoring sensors attached to the body. Results can be sent to other mobile devices worn by caregivers and physicians.[8]

Neuroscreen is a smartphone app that monitors Neurocognitive Impairment (NCI) in HIV-infected patients. NCI has serious medical and functional consequences, but screening for it is not routine and the condition often goes undiagnosed. Now patients can monitor their own health and NCI detection in time to address it with their doctors.

The Scanadu is a smaller-than-a-hockey-puck device that measures your heart rate and body temperature, performs an ECG, measures your blood oxygen levels, and twelve different signals in your urine to help you monitor your health effectively. Doctors or technicians are needed only to interpret the data and prescribe treatment. Reminiscent of the "Tricorder" from Star Trek, the Scanadu and devices appear to be the beginning of a technology revolution of the medical profession.

The medical field is also exploding with robot technology that targets cancer. Medical trials using nano-robots in humans have already started on leukemia patients. These robots are actually devices made from DNA and are injected into a patient's bloodstream with an ordinary medical syringe. The robot delivers a microscopic payload of drugs to kill cancer cells, repair spinal cord tissue, or seek out and alert your doctor to the presence of cancer cells before any other test can pick them up.[9]

What industries should pay attention to this trend in Internet-based medicine? Manufacturers of home testing kits and devices that must have samples taken and snail mailed in for diagnosis could see major changes in their industry. Companies who require drug-testing, on-site could process tests faster, or companies who offer

---

[8] http://nuviun.com/content/digital-health-in-action—smartphones-turn-into
-pointofcare-diagnostic-tools-for-mhealth#sthash.KxxSYHHg.dpuf

[9] http://www.dailymail.co.uk/sciencetech/article-3000904/Nanorobots-trial
-begin-humans-Microscopic-DNA-devices-injected-leukaemia-patient-bid-destroy
-abnormal-cells.html

mobile testing at a company's job site could expand their territory and offerings. Rural communities where people are often two to three hours away from a doctor's office could use their smartphones to get better, faster, more affordable care.

Non-Banks

You may not have noticed, but there are 5,439 fewer bank branches in 2015 than in 2008. Even the oldest and most well-known brick and mortar banks, like JPMorgan Chase, have announced retrenchment plans. America isn't leading the charge. In Europe the decline of branches is even faster.[10]

More customers are dependent on ATMs, smartphones, and banking online than they are on visiting a brick and mortar bank to talk to an agent. If bankers decide to imitate Apple, by having a few flagship stores around a region, and use technology to issue loans, approve mortgages and answer investment questions and transfers, how will your company be affected?

From merchant-oriented businesses like Square and PayPal to tech giants dabbling in payment services like Google Wallet and Apple Pay, there's increasing incentive for companies to offer money transfer services that exclude traditional banks entirely. In the wake of the 2008 financial crisis, the too-big-to-fail banks on Wall Street are still facing blowback from consumers everywhere. This kind of reception had to be something that giants like Citibank and Bank of America expected—what they couldn't have foreseen was the rise of the mobile payment system.

What started as a single, limited alternative to physical banking with PayPal has become a full-blown industry trend. Now that immensely familiar companies like Apple and Google are establishing direct relationships with customers over convenient, simple money

---

[10] http://www.economist.com/news/finance-and-economics/21650593-banks
-are-thinning-their-branch-networks-more-drastic-cuts-may-come-great?frsc=dg|a

transfers, what's to keep the banking industry from falling out of favor with American consumers?

Many of these services, like PayPal, effectively replace the function that banks serve in customers' lives. When you put money into accounts on these platforms, the money is left in that account and can be pulled back out from it — it's never handed off to a bank at any point for safekeeping.

And it's not just the business of hosting accounts that's being taken over, but the business of lending as well. Online services like Prosper let people lend money and take out loans without ever removing money from its completely online payment vehicle.

With trust in banking institutions rapidly declining and a youthful population that's more than comfortable turning their money over to companies without big metal vaults, it's hard not to see the threat this poses to the giants of Wall Street.

As BBVA's recent purchase of the banking startup Simple suggests the banking and finance sector is finding ways to integrate FinTech into it's traditional business.

The most important priority for companies in this industry should be enhancing and streamlining the consumer's digital experience of their brand. The average bank customer is getting less dependent on physical branches, so your company should do the same.

If banks can't assure that each of their clients will have just as easy of a time navigating their services from their homes as from one of their locations, they're going to struggle in the coming years.

Autonomous and Connected Vehicles

According to the National Highway Traffic Association, 94 percent of traffic accidents are caused by human error, making the argument for driverless cars stronger than ever. The primary causes of human error are alcohol, speed, and distracted rivers—things that aren't an issue for the driverless car. Connected cars are quite a few years from becoming commonplace, but they are out there. Google's driverless cars have driven 1.8 million miles in the last 6 years, and had only 12 minor accidents, none of which caused injuries and none that were the car's fault.

Elon Musk, the CEO and product architect for Tesla Motors, has announced that Tesla's much-hyped autonomous car will be ready to hit the pavement around 2020. Tesla expects these cars will be 10 times safer than those operated by actual people. If this estimate proves accurate, then we're talking about revolutionizing the way we get around every single day, a revolution Tesla will no doubt be driving front and center.

As simple as Musk makes it sound, however, there is no magic potion for a self-driving car, nor a simple process for making it a reality. Even once the necessarily amazing technology is fully developed and readily available, it will still take at least a few more years to overcome the inevitable legal obstacles. Someone needs to approve these driverless cars before we see them on the road. And that someone is inevitably the federal government. If competitors want even a puncher's chance at staying in the game, companies need to invest now in both the technology and the talented developers necessary to keep up with the top-notch innovation going on over at Tesla.

Autonomous driving will not only be applicable to individuals driving but also to public transportation such as buses, taxis, trains. The benefits to traditional businesses are already being realized including examples of Australian mining companies where driverless trucks are already being used to move coal in their operations.

America has 3.5 million truck drivers who account for an average of 5,000 deaths a year, almost 100 percent due to driver error.[11] What's not to like about that once the legal issues are resolved?

---

[11] http://zackkanter.com/2015/01/23/how-ubers-autonomous-cars-will-destroy-10-million-jobs-by-2025/

Few traditional automakers appear to be making moves towards the autonomous driving space which could leave them in a vulnerable position once driverless cars take off. [12] Autonomous driving will also have an impact on other traditional businesses tied to human driven cards, such as parking lots, automobile insurance, the automotive aftermarket, and autoparts stores as well as many forms of public transportation.

Drones

Unmanned flying machines drones range in size from the large planes used in long range surveillance intelligence and military operations to the small unmanned aerial systems (UAS) used by building inspectors to look over dangerous or slippery buildings, or insurance adjusters, fire and police officers who find it safer to inspect burned buildings, wrecks, and disaster sites from the air.

Until recently regulations and cost hampered the ownership of private drones. But regulations and the price of drones is changing. Predictions are that the number of private UAS owners will jump into the millions of owners range in less than a year, with various applications and disruptors to follow.

Look for personal drones to disrupt the real estate and property assessment markets, photography, and inspection of property and accident scenes, and agricultural markets. Drones will be able to spread pesticides, track escapees, look for lost, or missing persons and add law enforcement. Amazon is experimenting with drones for delivery of packages and the messenger bike services in large cities may also be impacted. Drug dealers are already using drones to cross the borders, but border patrols also use drones for monitoring such activity.[13]

---

[12] http://zackkanter.com/2015/01/23/how-ubers-autonomous-cars-will-destroy-10-million-jobs-by-2025/

[13] http://www.cnn.com/2015/01/22/world/drug-drone-crashes-us-mexico-border/

Virtual Reality

When Facebook spent $2 billion to acquire Oculus VR, the developer of the powerful, new, virtual-reality headset, Rift, they made a strong statement about where they see the future of digital going. Rift directly stimulates parts of the brain's visual cortex, immersing users in an engineered, hyper-reality that feels a little "matrix" like. With fully immersive goggles such as Oculus Rift, or see-through headgears like Hololens, customers will be able to immerse themselves into 3D virtual environments. Integral Reality (IR) weaves the wonders of digital within the physicality of real things. It embeds digital components, both the visible and invisible within objects, but rather than separate us from the real world, it promises to help us create emotionally engaging experiences with the world around us.[14]

The interesting challenge with virtual reality will be how to offer users natural ways to interact with virtual worlds. Consumers will want to handle objects and perform tasks like pointing, touching, grabbing, changing options, selecting, and purchasing. Therefore, companies in this space will need to think about things like motion, gesture, gaze, and voice recognition which will play important roles of offering natural users engagements.

The new VR/AR platforms will allow companies to dream up new interaction paradigms for content presentation, commerce, entertainment, educational, productivity, customer service, social and collaborative applications. This exciting experiential-immersion factor also introduces new ways for companies to envision how they can present users with engaging user experiences without the glass barriers of the current screens (i.e., computer monitors, mobile and tablet screens). Companies can also think about new interactions to trigger stronger emotional connections and more successful results between consumers and brands.

---

[14] http://www.wired.com/2014/08/the-war-for-our-digital-future/

Another virtual reality opportunity is the virtual retail shopping experience. Imagine shoppers will soon be able to walk through virtual stores, even pick up and examine merchandise, all from the comfort of their homes, and without having to stand in a line to check out. Knowledgeable clerks can even be available at the touch of a button to join the virtual walkthrough.

Biometric Identification

The average Internet user has 17 private passwords and 8.5 work passwords.[15] If that isn't bad enough, calling your bank, doctor's office, attorney or even your Internet provider can mean spending from 1 to 3 minutes authenticating yourself to the customer service center on the other end with secret passphrases and info. It's not the most positive way to begin your call, especially if you're one of the 75 percent who fail to identify and authenticate yourself the first time around.

Currently about 85 percent of customers find themselves unhappy and frustrated with their customer experiences connected to passwords. With customer services agents averaging one failed authentication every hour, a simple task turns the customer experience into an annoying, frustrating experience.

Enter voice biometrics (VB) and ballistocardiology. VB involves the identification of a person based on the unique characteristics of his or her voice and speech. Ballistocardiology is the study of the activity of the heart and the body's movement. Such movement creates unique data and a biometric print that could be used as a unique password.

Both ballistocardiology and voiceprints are more distinctive than fingerprints, with more than 90 percent accuracy. Customers who experience a more positive interaction with a company because of VB are more likely to use self-service options again rather than turn

---

[15] http://www.wired.com/2014/08/the-war-for-our-digital-future/

to a live operator for assistance. Expect to see different kinds of biometrics used for everything from voter registration to ATM or bank withdrawals, to check-ins at work, airports, or for security purposes. "By 2017, passive biometric analysis will become a standard feature of at least 30 percent of one-stop fraud detection solutions - up from less than 1 percent today." wrote Gartner analyst, Avivah Litan in Gartner's *Market Guide for Online Fraud Detection*.[16] This is definitely a trend to be watching.

Paperless and Cashless

Paper is not only wasteful, but inefficient. You can't search for information by keywords on paper like you can on digital. You have to store, protect, and organize paper files. You can't email paper or the information on it, unless you first scan it. Even if you scan it, the paper remains and must be shredded or refiled. Paper documents must be physically delivered or mailed, making receiving the information and document time dependent. There is no instantaneous delivery. So why do banks and institutions, utilities, and other companies continue to default to paper delivery?

The common belief is that people resist paperless because it is the default option for so many people and organizations that grew up with it. Experts say paperless hasn't fully taken hold because of a lack of rock-solid, secure technology—especially at the signature or date stamping layer. The technology must be able to date-stamp data and verifying its authenticity, something that has only recently become available in what is called Keyless Signature Infrastructure (KSI) which allows for the security and verifiable signing and dating of financial, legal, and medical files.[17]

---

[16] https://www.gartner.com/doc/2756017/market-guide-online-fraud-detection

[17] http://insights.wired.com/profiles/blogs/dematerialization-with-disrupt-all -industries#axzz3hw2mriwO

It's probably not going to be a law that will change our monetary system. More likely it will be the use of wearables, biometrics, and smartphone technology that turns our phones into electronic wallets that may hasten the demise of cash.

Acuity Market Intelligence (AMI) reports that mobile biometrics, with or without a mobile device or wearable, will generate $34.6 billion in annual revenue in 2020, significantly disrupting the global payment market by providing alternative means of securing and processing mobile transactions. Biometrics will lower both the risk and cost of payment processing. AMI projects biometrics will be used to authenticate nearly 65 percent of all m-Commerce (mobile commerce) transactions in 2020. This represents 126 billion biometric payment transactions generating more than $1.1 trillion in consumer mCommerce purchase value.

Banks take note. Biometric-based real-time risk assessment will also transform payment processing allowing consumers to withdraw funds directly from consumer bank and mobile money accounts via their mobile devices while enabling merchants to issue direct consumer credit on demand. This has the potential to totally disrupt traditional payment methods, such as credit and debit cards. Acuity forecasts that the total biometric transaction volume, including both payment and nonpayment transactions, will exceed 800 million annually by 2020 with 35 percent of these transactions authenticated via biometrics embedded in mobile devices and 65 percent via biometric apps downloaded by consumers.[18]

Wi-Fi And Wireless Power Duo

Most of the digital technology devices we use today, from laptops, to wearables, to smartphones to drones, is battery powered. It doesn't matter how sophisticated your device is. When it's out of battery power, it stops. It's the laws of physics, not the lack of innovation

---

[18] http://www.acuity-mi.com/

that slowing innovation in the ability of batteries to keep up with the increasing complexity of apps and the demands of sophisticated and powerful smartphone cameras. The physics of batteries may currently limit the distance and performance of technology, but wireless battery charging could change all that. Nikola Tesla was the first to dream of a world of wireless power transmission, but never lived to see it happen. However, this generation will most likely see Tesla's wireless power vision in action.

Philips, the large electronics manufacturer, has demonstrated a cordless food processor powered by a coil sunk into a counter, and other companies, like Starbucks and McDonalds, are already offering wireless charging for customers.[19] Charging smartphones will be a major convenience for consumers; however, the opportunity for wireless power will have a dramatic impact at the industrial level.

A commercial-grade wireless charging product capable of replacing the numerous wired power connections for sensors and monitors in sensitive facilities like oil and gas refineries is on the horizon.[20]

Wirelessly powered devices in commercial applications decrease fire and explosion risks by minimizing the number of potential opportunities there are for generating sparks. With fewer live cables lying around the workplace is safer. Wireless charging will disrupt the battery industry and potentially the power cord industry as wireless power, like Wi-Fi, can go through walls and around corners.[21]

While wireless charging will make mobile devices more reliable, the growth in Wi-Fi could be the perfect compliment to this trend. Smartphones aren't going away, but cell towers might. A string of wireless startups are betting that over the next few years, mobile phones will switch to sending most calls, texts, and data via Wi-Fi hotspots,

---

[19] http://www.economist.com/news/science-and-technology/21656134
-electronics-has-already-cut-data-cord-can-it-now-cut-power-cord
#c1wuOhKlJbWZQ3kZ.99

[20] http://techcrunch.com/2013/09/09/cota-by-ossia-wireless-power/

[21] http://techcrunch.com/2013/09/09/cota-by-ossia-wireless-power/

relegating the cellular network to being a mere backup. Once the 5G networks that can latch onto Wi-Fi roll out in the coming year, there's likely to be more attention paid to Wi-Fi over cellular.[22]

Robotics

Robots are finally on the verge of revolutionizing humankind. From manufacturing plants to military environments and eventually in our homes and offices, in the next decade we will experience what until recently only science fiction could offer. If you have not yet experienced interacting with the new generation of humanoid robots that are being developed in Japan by companies like Honda—you are in for a shock. They can walk, talk, hear, see and interact in ways that will be overwhelming to many people.

Industrial robots, which have been replacing workers in manufacturing environments for years, are now starting to take an extreme foothold around the world. They are becoming more cost effective than ever, and as a result have experienced a dramatic increase in adoption worldwide by many manufacturers and distributors. They can also provide more sophisticated functionality than ever before—like picking and packing, and most recently sewing.

Until now sewing has been a uniquely human task, requiring hands and people to perform the surprisingly complex actions needed to sew two pieces of material together. It's been impossible for machines to align, feed, and constantly adjust fabric to prevent it slipping and buckling, while all the time keeping the stitches neat and the thread at the right tension.[23]

Enter the robotic sewing machine—changing how we produce clothing, but more importantly eliminating millions of jobs and

---

[22] http://www.economist.com/news/business/21654602-wi-fi-first-technology -will-be-great-consumers-disruptive-mobile-firms-change#5GKeo7L9yrUYRqVg.99

[23] http://www.economist.com/news/business/21654602-wi-fi-first-technology -will-be-great-consumers-disruptive-mobile-firms-change#5GKeo7L9yrUYRqVg.99

thousands of sweatshops around the world. Nike is already using a machine that weaves polyester yarn into the shape of the upper part of its running shoes. It was just a matter of time before technology was devised to sew jeans, pants, shirts, and skirts.

Expect worldwide replacement of sweatshops, transportation, manufacturing, retail, and even in the design and fabrics industry as machines will be able to create intricate clothing designs that will push high-end fashion into the affordable range. New fabrics and combinations of fabrics that adapt better to sewing robots will disrupt the fashion industry.

There has also been a new generation of "collaborative" robots recently integrated into manufacturing facilities that work and train with humans on a daily basis. They can actually learn from their "human coworkers" by observing physical demonstrations of tasks.

Robotics may be the one of the ultimate manifestations of digital transformation. As robots become increasingly accepted in society they will contribute to the acceleration of digital transformation that occurs in our lives at work and at home. How far and how fast digital technology will change society, the economy, and the environment is still unknown, but as robotics, AI, big data, and the Internet continue to converge, be aware that nothing is impossible.

Technology will continue to evolve, and so will the things people will need and want. We will always want to be clothed, fed, sheltered, entertained, and connected. And technology will continue to advance to ensure that happens faster, cheaper, better, and with the most amazing customer experience possible. Remember, the Industrial Revolution began from a desire for something as simple as providing a way to make fabric faster and cheaper. We're still finding ways to clothe ourselves faster and cheaper. Digital transformation and industrial revolutions are ultimately about people, not just technology. It takes technology to achieve the advances, but ultimately it all comes down to the consumer's experience and your ability to provide the best experience ever. Are you ready to do that?

Index

Index

Note: Page numbers followed by f represent figures.